A. H. Williams. 1926.

CHURCH AND STATE
IN THE MIDDLE AGES

THE FORD LECTURES
DELIVERED AT OXFORD IN 1905

By A. L. SMITH

BALLIOL COLLEGE, OXFORD

OXFORD
AT THE CLARENDON PRESS
1913

OXFORD UNIVERSITY PRESS

LONDON   EDINBURGH   GLASGOW   NEW YORK
TORONTO   MELBOURNE   BOMBAY

HUMPHREY MILFORD M.A.
PUBLISHER TO THE UNIVERSITY

LECTURE I

THE Papacy as a working institution; new documents available for its study. The two sides of its history contrasted. (1) Its civilizing influence; (2) the growth of bitter feeling against it. The English ' No Popery ' view, not merely due to the Reformation, though the Reformation does have its roots deep in the past; the causes were at work as early as 1250, along with very opposite influences.

The subject of the lectures therefore is, The good and evil of the connexion of England with Rome, especially in the middle of the thirteenth century.

LECTURE I. The effects of this connexion upon the English Church, as shown in—

(1) The Legatine constitutions of 1237, and their most important articles. Comparison of these with the long series of English canons, the affiliation of these latter and the general evidence which they supply.

(2) The Gemma Ecclesiastica, its limitations and its general character; its thaumaturgy shows that the Church did not create but did control superstition; the abuses, ignorance, slackness, and immorality among the clergy; the influence of Papal central power.

(3) Grosseteste's letters, as confirmatory evidence; also his own constitutions.

(4) In the Burton Annals, the Coventry visitation gives the same picture. The Berkshire rectors' protest examined; very outspoken, but containing no attack on the Papal *plenitudo potestatis*.

(5) The commentary of John Athon, later in date but may be used; his criticisms on the English clergy; his acceptance of the Pope's supremacy and judicial and dispensing powers.

(6) The Papal Register: its historical value as authentic, contemporary, genuine, careful, and representative. It shows (a) the ordinary administration of the Papacy, and the effect of its central decisions; the good and evil of Rome's influence; the monasteries as needing the help of Rome and the control by Rome. The evidence from the Bulls issued to Grosseteste. (b) The abnormal features under Innocent IV, pluralities, &c. (c) The normal administration turned to partisan purposes.

(7) The Papacy as an appeal court; the causes of its development, (i) especially in England; (ii) appeals a gravamine; (iii) a choice between anarchy and centralization; (iv) it did not imply foreign judges; (v) the resort to Rome for advice; (vi) the Pope as *iudex ordinarius*. The prejudices about canon law apply to its later stages; the ideal aimed at in the system was a kingdom of God on earth. Can such a system be entrusted to ordinary men ? Can religion be made a system, without detriment to it ?

(8) The confessional; Innocent III's rule of confession; its later results, to make obedience the one virtue, to make a tariff of penances, to centre the aims of the Church on clerical domination, to develop casuistry. Yet the objects of the rule had been noble, and its first effects good, including further centralization.

LECTURE II

Syllabus

THE action of the Papacy upon English social life, illustrated from the province of the law of marriage.

Mediaeval Church views seem unpleasing on marriage ; but had great difficulties due to rival law codes, and to Scriptural texts, in bringing principle into a chaos of Jewish, Roman, and Teutonic traditions. (1) Why the Church was timid as to the sacramental view of marriage, and never insisted on the presence of a clerk in orders for the validity of marriage ; case of dower and other divergences from Church law show (*a*) a growing hostility of secular lawyers ; (*b*) less spirituality and less tolerance on their part. (2) How distinction of *praesenti* and *futuro* arose ; argument of Peter Lombard ; practical results, e. g. on infant betrothals ; Paris versus Bologna ; Pope required as arbiter, and the law approaches certitude. The Papacy also checks extremists and enforces compromise, and raises a presumption in favour of marriage, and insists that only the Papacy can declare voidances. (3) How rule as to affinity arose, though modified in practice, especially by Papacy as to degrees of affinity. The Papacy restricts the principle also of spiritual affinity even if created by the confessional. Relation of local customs to Papal authority. (4) Papal decisions as to marriages with heathen, as to adultery, widows, prohibited seasons. The motive of these rules as to consanguinity and affinity ; the more lax the practice, the higher the ideal. (5) Struggle between the Papacy and the canonists on the vow of celibacy ; can the Pope dispense from such a vow ? The *votum simplex* and *votum solemne*. Clerical celibacy a necessary stage in history ; growth of the theory, collides with the theory of Papal *plenitudo potestatis*. (6) Divorce ; it took the Church eleven centuries to make marriage indissoluble ; but this rule collides with monasticism. Papal compromises on this and on other questions. (7) Development of Pope's dispensing power, despite practical limitations, up to Boniface VIII ; acceptance of it in England in the thirteenth century compared with the twelfth ; its value. (8) Were the Reformers quite fair to the canon law ? Is it fair to describe all this law as ' a game of skill ', ' a maze of flighty fancies ', something which outweighs ' all the merits of the mediaeval Church ' ? Which was more to blame, the mediaeval Church or mediaeval society itself ?

Summary. Importance of Papacy as final appeal, as peacemaker among canonists, as representing workable compromise, as protecting the marriage tie. It can only be judged in its historical setting and working.

LECTURE III

Syllabus

THE hold of the Papacy upon the best minds of the age. The Papacy as a Church-State a rival of the lay State ; their relation in the thirteenth century. Grosseteste's view of the Pope as the head of the Church-State, contrasted with his famous letter and with Matthew Paris's picture of him, will show (a) the hold which the Papacy had, (b) how and why that hold began to relax.

Examination of the letter (not written to the Pope) ; its peculiarities in style and argument ; compared with his other letters, e. g. to Cardinal Otto, to the Pope, and to the King, which show complete submission to Papal orders. Could the writer of these have written that one ? It closely resembles typical mediaeval ' forgeries ', such as those attributed to the Emperor Frederick. Grosseteste's conduct in other parallel cases ; his watchword ' rebellion is as the sin of witchcraft.' The letter is part of a group of documents and events ; (1) the dialogue between Pope and Cardinals. (2) Grosseteste's death-bed speeches, which profess to be his voice but the hand is the hand of Matthew Paris. (3) Do contemporaries support the letter ? (4) Why is it not in his collected letters ? (5) The story of a Papal rebuff to Grosseteste in 1250 very suspicious as told in Matthew Paris. (6) His sermon to Pope and Cardinals, its great interest and conclusions to be drawn from it ; Matthew Paris's account of its results and story of Grosseteste's suspension and his estimate of Papal exactions. (7) Papal answers of May and November 1253. (8) The letter to English laity, certainly not Grosseteste's. (9) Story of Grosseteste being excommunicated is unsupported.

But even without the suspicious documents some general conclusions may be drawn : (a) the great hold which the Papacy still had on England ; (b) the intense Papalism of the best men ; (c) the breach made by Innocent IV ; (d) the untrustworthiness of Matthew Paris with all his merits.

Mediaeval unity, compared with modern disunion, despite some tendencies to reunion. Causes of modern acquiescence in this condition ; prejudices which obscure our view. Is it safe to say that ' all has been for the best ' ? Or need the Reformation have come just in the way it did ? Have we lost nothing in the process ? Has not a theory like Grosseteste's the interest of a challenge to us ?

LECTURE IV

SYLLABUS

THE movement against the Papacy ; the crucial years 1246–54 added Provisions to Papal Taxes. The English grievances at Lyons, chiefly touch Taxation : the Pope's answer, renewed protest by clergy and the exact bearing of this protest on the theory of Papalism. The protest of Louis IX, its remarkable line of argument ; its admissions explain why the Reformation did not come for nearly three centuries ; character of the protest, and its date 1247, not 1245 as Matthew Paris thought ; its complaints verified from the Papal Registers, showing vast growth of abuses under Innocent IV. Contrast of the English and French positions. Immovableness of the Pope despite new protests from English laity and clergy, 1247. ' Unheard of ' grants to Archbishop Boniface ; complicity of Henry III, his vow of crusade. Papal attitude about Provisions, 1247–8, as reflected in the Registers and in the cases given by Matthew Paris.

General conclusions as to results, 1245–50, the death of the Emperor Frederick—

1. The practical effect of Provisions, why they were so hated. Even Innocent IV has to temporize.
2. The complete acceptance nevertheless of the *plenitudo potestatis* ; this explains the Papal inflexibility.
3. The contrast between the position of Louis IX and that of Henry III ; England ' the milch cow of the Papacy '.
4. Innocent IV's pontificate constitutes an epoch ; the idea of appeal to a Council.

Critical examination of Matthew Paris as the general authority on this period ; his personal character ; in many ways, though not all, a typical Englishman and a typical man of his time. How he has come to dominate English history ; the varying worth of his testimony ; it needs to be sifted. But does he give an adequate picture of the Papacy as (*a*) a spiritual power, or (*b*) a political power ?

It is necessary to test him

1. As a monastic chronicler ; state of the Benedictine Order in the thirteenth century ; his attitude to general Church aims of the time and to the Friars.
2. As a censor of the Papacy ; the grounds of his opposition ; its inconsistencies and onesidedness.
3. As a political partisan ; his aristocratic sympathies, his dislike of centralization, his lack of constitutional insight.
4. His omissions and defects ; his want of great ideas, his discontents, his want of true critical faculty ; his textual carelessness ; finally, is he always honest and scrupulous ?

LECTURE V

SYLLABUS

THE general belief that the middle of the thirteenth century was to be a new epoch in the history both of the Church and the world ; ' the age of the Holy Ghost was to begin as predicted by the holy abbot Joachim ' (Salimbene). Meaning of this Joachimite persuasion.

Henry III and the Papacy, especially (A) from the English side, 1250–8. Mediaeval principle of commutations, now applied to crusading vows for the benefit of Henry III ; his closer alliance with Rome, 1250; its objects, e. g. Aymer in the see of Winchester ; similar cases, 1250–3, Henry's retort ; climax of the alliance is the offer of Sicilian crown to Earl Richard, 1247 (?) and 1250 and 1252 ; his wary refusal ; but Henry III accepts ; his debts and struggles, 1253–8, and final renunciation of it, 1258, but not till it had caused the national revolt of 1258–65.

The same relations (B) from the Papal side, 1250–4. Innocent III's policy, to create the Papal States, taken up by Innocent IV ; it led him to attempt the conquest of Sicily, 1248, by Cardinal Peter ; his successes, 1249 ; then complete recovery of power by Frederick, 1250 ; Innocent recalls Cardinal Peter, makes advances to Earl Richard ; the Emperor's death, December 1250, on the eve of final victory ; importance of his death ; Innocent's scheme revived at once, 1251, but failed again, 1252 ; he lets the peace party try a settlement with Conrad, January–June 1252 ; on their failure, Sicily is offered both to Earl Richard, in November 1252, and to Charles of Anjou, who draws back at the last moment, October 1253 ; Innocent has to surrender again to the peace party at a heavy cost ; his objects in this and his double dealing with England ; the part played by Thomas of Savoy ; Innocent was on the eve of humiliation to Conrad IV when the king dies suddenly, May 1254.

Reflections on the great duel of Papacy and Empire ; the relation of Church and State ought not to be hostile ; they have the same end by different means ; the mediaeval failure due to their passion to realize their ideals and to embody them ; of this both Papacy and Empire are instances, but the mistake was greater in (a) turning the Church into a State, (b) adding the ever widening idea of Papal States, for this proved a fatal legacy. But in the great duel the Empire must fall ; even Frederick could only have postponed the day ; for (i) his was not a real Empire and not Roman ; (ii) the head of Christendom must be the Pope ; (iii) his unpardonable sins were his claim to rule Rome, his hold over the Matildine lands, his menace to the Papal allies the Lombards, and his being king of Naples. In the struggle he was more honest than Innocent IV, but the Papacy still represented higher ideals than the Empire in many ways. Yet, but for Innocent IV, the Empire might have gone on awhile, and (i) continued the experiment of an orderly tolerant centralized government in South Italy, (ii) continued to produce great results from the idea of Christendom, (iii) continued to aim at a noble vision, the co-operation of the two swords, the Caesar and the Apostle.

LECTURE VI

I. Papal position in May 1254 ; Conrad's will ; Henry III's acceptance of Sicily ; rising in Sicily against Germans and the meaning of this. Submission of Manfred ; Innocent's mistake in despising him, Manfred's revolt ; Innocent's double dealing with England, total defeat of his army by Manfred and collapse of Papal designs on Sicily for the fourth time since 1247. The Papacy clung to his design and was only saved by the deaths of Manfred in 1266 and Conradin in 1268, and even so fell into Angevin bondage and the seventy years' Captivity, a contrast to ' the kingdom of God on earth ',

II. Innocent IV tested by his dealings with the German Church. His treatment of bishoprics, ' irregularities ', crusaders ; ' purging ' the chapters ; provisors, pluralities. This is what he meant by ' a spiritual war '. He earned his success. But was it success ? Note the resentment of the laity, still more that of different sections of clergy, the prelates, the universities, the reforming party, even the Friars and monks.

III. Estimate of the personal character of Innocent IV ; his relations to the Cardinals ; his nepotism ; comparison with his three predecessors ; his prevision ; his worldly wisdom ; his self-control ; the greatest power on earth was at last in the hands of a consummate man of business ; evidence of the Registers ; his power of adaptation ; his command of diplomacy, instances from the biography ; his selection of agents and use of them ; his condescension to men's weaknesses ; his use of the Friars and of the ideas of his age. Above all he put the Papacy on a financial basis ; views of contemporaries and of his biographer on this. His attitude to culture and art as compared with Frederick II. His sublime self-confidence. ' The Church must win.' But did he win ? Did ' the Church ' win ?

LECTURE I

PAPAL INFLUENCES IN THE ENGLISH CHURCH OF THE EARLIER THIRTEENTH CENTURY

DURING the last fifty or sixty years the study of history has been passing through a change which amounts to a revolution. Its sources are now not so much the contemporary chronicles as the contemporary documents. Vast masses of these have been collected, critically sifted, and calendared. Take the greatest institution in history, the Papacy—take it at the most creative and decisive period in the modern world, the first half of the thirteenth century. There are now available for the study of this institution during that time the Registers of the Empire and the Registers of the Papacy itself. The former comprise 14,800 documents ; the latter more than 8,000 for the one pontificate of Innocent IV, a period of eleven and a half years.

New sources for history of the Papacy.

No one except a person shielded from the painful impact of new ideas by proof armour of sectarian prejudice could rise from even a cursory study of these records without feeling two powerful, if contrasted, impressions. On the one hand, he must be profoundly stirred to admiration of the machinery and organization of the Papacy ; its

enormous superiority, not merely as a religious
centre, but as the centre of law and government ;
its all-pervading activity and almost infinite
potentialities ; and, finally, the absolute and
literal acceptance of it by the highest minds as
the veritable oracle and tribunal of God. On the
other hand, there will be an impression as deep,
of the abuses, so unconcealed yet so long endured,
which ate into the very heart of the system ;
of the narrow selfishness and wholly political
character of its most cherished aim, the aim of
a petty territorial princedom in Italy ; of its
increasing concentration upon this one aim, till
phrases such as ' the Church ', ' the Faith ', and
' the cause of God ', came to mean this petty aim
and this alone ; and, finally, of the growing bitterness and even outspoken invective which it aroused
in all countries and all classes.

This bitterness is familiar to us in the Reformers
of the sixteenth century, or in the Puritans of
the seventeenth, but the following passage is from
a treatise of 1735.

The Eng-　' A certain set of men . . . did set up and for many ages
lish　cry maintain a kingdom of their own over the greatest part
of ' No
Popery ' of the Christian world ; the most impious and oppressive
tyranny that ever exercised the patience of God or man ;
an Empire founded in craft and supported by blood and
rapine, breach of faith, and every other engine of fraud
and oppression.'

This represents not unfairly the spirit in which
the average Englishman still continues to approach

what was at any rate the greatest institution in
human history. He has not consciously formulated
his opinion ; perhaps he would not give it such
robust expression ; but the softening would be
from decorum rather than from lack of conviction.
' No Popery ' has vanished from our walls and our
hoardings, but the truculent old watchword is
still written large across our historical perspective.
Yet among the first lessons taught us by any
honest study of the past, is that the force of
criticism is often in inverse proportion to violence
of language, and that prejudice is worse than a
crime—it is a blunder and a waste of time. We
cannot frame an indictment against a whole era,
and history refuses to be packed into epigrams or
distorted into philippics. Nor will any one who
has followed even in outline the story of a Gregory
the Great, a Hildebrand, an Innocent III, be
willing to dismiss them as ' a set of men who
maintained an impious and oppressive tyranny ' ;
or willing to admit that this great spiritual empire
of which St. Augustine was the architect required
nothing but craft for its foundations ; or that the
Church of Grosseteste and St. Francis had nothing
but blood, rapine, and fraud for its supports.
How came it, then, that the mere name of Popery
should stir to such a rabid pitch a mind from which
we might expect judicial calm ? *Tantaene animis
caelestibus irae ?* For the author of the treatise
was no less a man than Sir Michael Foster, Chief

Justice of the King's Bench, a man eulogized by
Blackstone and Thurlow, and apostrophized by
another chief justice a generation later as 'an
embodied Magna Carta of persons as of fortunes'.
The usual explanation given to account for the
depth and perennial flow of this stream of anti-
papal feeling in England takes some such form
as the following : The Reformation was no
sudden cataclysm ; it has its sources far back in
our history. Wiclif, Boniface VIII, the vassalage
of King John, the Constitutions of Clarendon,
William the Conqueror's refusal to hold his
kingdom as a papal fief—these are the familiar
landmarks pointed out to us as we retrace the
movement of resistance against Rome back to
not sole- its fountain-heads. To make for our path a plain
ly due to
the Re- beaten way many powerful influences have con-
forma-
tion. tributed. There is the influence of insular patriotism,
which so often forgets that to be an island and to
be insular need not be equally good things. There
is the influence of Anglicanism, with its claim of
independence for the national Church and its
protests against ' Papal encroachments '. There
is the stubborn spirit of the layman, which even
in the ages of faith often blazed up against sacerdotalism. Lastly, an easy way seems to have
been made for us by the work of generations of
lawyers, from Glanvil down to living ex-Chan-
cellors, who have always been jealous for Westminster against Canterbury, and more jealous

than ever when Canterbury was backed by
Rome.

But though each of the five main aspects of the
Reformation movement may assuredly be traced
back into the thirteenth century, and some of them
even into the eleventh century, yet we must
beware of thinking that those centuries' chief
occupation was to prepare for the Reformation.
Such a caution is by no means superfluous. For
in modern times, and especially in the most
modern, when it can be said truly that we are
all historians now, we can hardly help falling into
the habit of what is called ' reading history back
wards '. Knowing what did happen, by a kind
of historical fatalism we assume that it was the
only thing which could have happened. More
than this, we assume that everything which did
not obviously help it to happen may be relegated
to a limbo of things which themselves only half
happened. Familiar as we are with the *dénouement*
of the great drama, we tend to toss aside as an
interruption everything that does not forward the
central plot, to dismiss all else as side-issues,
irrelevancies, blind alleys.

We even go so far as to regard the whole of
mediaeval Church history as an introduction to
the Reformation, and treat all appearances to
the contrary as superficial and misleading ; all
forces which tend the other way are factors which
may be neglected, like the weight of the elephant

in the mathematical problem. Certainly this would make history very convenient for the personage who calls himself the plain man, but is it quite so satisfactory in other respects when the factors which we have neglected force themselves at last on our attention ? If we could absolutely divest ourselves of prejudice, if we could approach the greatest century of the Middle Ages with an open mind, we should soon find two propositions taking shape before our eyes, and one notable inference resulting therefrom.

The problem of Papal history. 1. The Papacy, taking it all in all, was the greatest potentiality for good that existed at the time, or perhaps that has ever existed.

2. During the first part of the thirteenth century the hold which the Papacy had on Christendom was still increasing ; whereas half-way through the century the loss of that hold had become a foregone conclusion, and the only question left was, How long would it take for the crash to come ?

3. The resulting inference is that herein lies our problem : To analyse and to explain the momentous change which came about in the interval between the death of Innocent III and the death of Innocent IV. To locate the problem within closer limits, let us take the pontificate of Innocent IV for our time, and let us take England for our place.

Accordingly the heads under which my subject

naturally ranges itself are as follows : The in- Papal
fluence of the Papacy (i) on the English Church, influences
and (ii) on English social life, especially during upon
thir-
the early thirteenth century. (iii) The exact teenth-
century
nature and extent of this influence, as tested in England.
the case of the greatest English churchman of
that time.

Then turning to the other side of the medal,
the dealings between England and the Papacy
during this pontificate, (iv) from the English, and
(v) from the Papal side.

Finally, (vi) the character of Innocent IV, and
the precise nature of the general policy which so
irrevocably committed the Papacy to its downward
path.

I. To observe the actual working of the Papacy The Legatine
on the English Church, it will be most convenient Council
to place ourselves at a particular occasion—the of 1237.
occasion of the visit to England of the Legate
Otto, Cardinal Bishop of Palestrina. He was in
England from June 29, 1237, till January 12,
1241 ; and in December 1237 he held his famous
council at London.

Almost the sole authority for his legation is
Matthew Paris, an authority which must be
discounted in this matter, for he never allows that
a Legate was needed at all. If we read only what
he says about the Legate, we should come away
with the idea that the visit had no other aim than
to extort money, and no other origin than some

superstitious hankerings on the part of Henry III.
But while telling us of the fifty fat oxen, the hundred measures of wheat, the eight casks of choice
wine, which were the Bishop of Winchester's
present to the Legate, and of the King's seeming
to worship the Legate's very footprints, he yet
admits that Otto had a high character for holiness,
fama sancti, the King of Scots said, and Scottish
standards of sanctity are proverbially high.
Matthew Paris, moreover, admits that the Legate
acquired great esteem by a general refusal of other
gifts.   We have also the articles of Otto's Council
to show the urgent need of reform in the English
Church, besides Otto's announcement that he had
come to restore the Church to the honourable position from which it had fallen.[1]   Moreover, in the
account which Matthew Paris gives of the bold
stand taken by Walter of Cantelupe, Bishop of
Worcester, there is no attempt to disguise the
character of the opposition to the *immutator
regni* ; it stands confessed an outcry of pluralists
and illegitimate holders.   ' Many like ourselves of
noble blood ', says the candid bishop, ' hold plural
benefices ; if we are to be deprived of one, we will
resign them all in a body.'

The re-   It has been said above that the articles of the
forms at-
tempted. Council show the need of a reform.   These are the
articles in brief :

---

[1] M. Paris, *Chronica Maiora*, iv, p. 418 ; *casum* is softened to
statum in John of Athon.

1. Churches must be consecrated within two years from the time of their completion, or else mass must not be said therein.

2. Priests are ignorant as to the proper conduct of the sacraments.

3. Folk are reluctant on superstitious grounds to be baptized at Lent and at Pentecost.

4. Sacraments are refused till money is paid.

5. Parsons are ashamed to confess to their rural deans.

6. Orders are conferred on bastards, on men with no title, &c.

7. Churches are farmed out, as is also the case with deaneries and the offices of archdeacons, &c.

8. Vicars are appointed at a mere pittance, and

9. often from men who are below deacons' orders.

10. Benefices are held by force on rumour of the incumbent's death.

11. Orders are often given to a man who seems *miles non clericus*.

12. Non-residents and pluralities are rife.

13. Short coats are worn by clerks, and close caps are avoided.

14. Clerks are married in secret, and

15. the sons of such marriages succeed to the benefices.

16. Maintainers of robbers are suffered, who ought to be excommunicated.

17. Mere novices are made abbots.

18. The archdeacons are venal and oppressive.

19. Bishops are non-resident and inactive.

20. The Church suffers from ignorant ecclesiastical judges.

21. Evasions and sham citations are practised in ecclesiastical suits.

22. Frauds and injustices are caused by there being no notaries in England.

23. Advocates in ecclesiastical courts ought to be bound by oath to plead fairly.

24. Records ought to be kept of the suits in these courts.

When Matthew Paris sums up the feelings of the clergy after this indictment : ' *Cum parvo gaudio recesserunt,*' we are reminded of the rich young man in the Gospel, who went away sorrowful.

The impulse came from Rome. These canons of Otto, like those precedent and those subsequent to his Legation, are the outcome of one source, and that source is Rome. Thus much might be proved in other ways, even if the circumstances of each issue of canons had not come down to us. Otto's canons agree closely with the law of the Church, as it was by now established in the Decretals and accepted by the commentators. From their writings come the copious citations with which Athon backs up his edition of Otto's constitutions, in which he glosses literally every word, the scantiest rivulet of text meandering through meadows of luxuriant commentary. Otto's canons expressly follow the matter and often the wording of the Lateran Council of 1216. Thus Langton's prohibition of fees for baptism or other sacraments expressly refers for further instructions to the Lateran decree (§ 66) ; and again, Otto's order (§ 19) that bishops are to repeat their vows twice a year is found earlier in Langton, but comes from the Lateran decree. The chief points in Otto's canons are just the points that the Papacy had been taking to heart as the peculiar vices of England.

These articles are of very various weight. They range from trifles (e.g. §§ 1, 13) to crimes (§§ 14, 15, 16) ; but in each and all, their testimony is confirmed by a number of different witnesses. The English diocesan and provincial canons, both precedent and posterior, bear out Otto's canons as Legate. So does Giraldus's lively work called the *Gemma Ecclesiastica* ; so too the long series of Grosseteste's letters ; so the interesting documents in the Burton Annals ; and so also John of Athon, the first manual of canon law for English use. All these works supply evidence as to the nature and value of the Papal influence on the English Church, which I propose also to illustrate by a summary analysis of the Papal Registers, by a brief sketch of the Papacy as a court of appeal, and by some estimate of Innocent III's new rule for the confessional.

Otto's constitutions of 1237 are borne out by provincial and diocesan canons. The first that Lyndwood allows in his collection are Langton's canons of 1222 ; and these are largely a transcript from the Lateran Council of 1216, at which Langton was present. They end with an instruction for the Lateran canons to be read yearly in each bishop's synod. The subjects Langton omits are those which needed the wider powers of a Legate *a latere* : the illegitimate sons of priests succeeding to benefices ; the non-residence of bishops ; and the defective working of the Church courts. Those of Edmund Rich, 1236, are only diocesan, and are also largely drawn from the Lateran decrees of 1216, even to the extent of borrowing the technical term *vidom*, which was meaningless in England (§ 34). They are nearly as stringent as Otto's, but of course had none of his coercive power ; and for that reason they touch neither the courts nor the archdeacons, nor many of the most serious points.

The canons of Durham (probably about 1222, under Bishop Richard Marsh) profess to carry out Langton's canons, and are nearly the same.[1] Thus the eighth paragraph, dealing with incontinent priests, refers for fuller details to the Archbishop's rules, and warns subordinate prelates not to go on neglecting them for pecuniary gain. Another paragraph republishes almost verbatim

[1] Wilkins, *Concilia*, i. 572.

the recent order of the Lateran Council of 1216,
which enjoined annual confession.

There is in existence a set of canons for Coventry
diocese ; they are dated 1237, but are evidently
prior to those of Otto, and curiously timid in their
attitude to clerical sinners.   For incontinency
a priest on the first two convictions is to be
fined only.

'We fine in money because men fear money penalties
most, and because it is wealth that is the cause of wanton-
ness. . . . But for all our threats of excommunication we
fear they will not return to the Lord, for the spirit of
uncleanness is among them.'

A priest who frequents scot-ales, who haunts
taverns, or is a tavern-keeper, gets off with a fine
of 6s. 8d. The only offence which is firmly handled
is that of a layman striking a clerk ; for such a deed
the culprit must go to Rome for absolution, unless
he be at the very point of death.

There were evidently many such sets of diocesan
canons issued.   One and all show the same evils
in the English Church, and the same reliance on
Rome as the only ultimate source to which men
might look for reform.   Or let us reverse the glass,
and consider the movement not locally, but from
the centre. The Registers of Honorius III show
a steady pressure from the Papacy during these
years to keep the English Church alive to its
own gravest abuses, namely, the married clergy,

and the priests' sons succeeding to their fathers' benefices.[1]

So the canons evoked by Council of Lyons.

Just as the earlier crop of provincial canons are the outcome of the great Lateran Council of 1216, so there is a later crop (1246, 1250, 1255) produced by the Council of Lyons, besides the intermediate crop from Otto's Legatine visit of 1237. Of this latest series some canons are preserved only in fragments ; of the two which remain in full, the Statuta of Richard de la Wych, Bishop of Chichester, 1246, expressly repeat the Legatine statutes of 1237 ; for example, in ordering married priests to dismiss their wives within a month, on pain of suspension. They also insist that monks shall obey the rules laid down in Gregory IX's decretals. The Statutes of William de Kirkham, Bishop of Durham, 1255, enact that the statutes of his late predecessor, Bishop Richard, are to endure in full force ; and also explain that these precedent statutes are republished now because they have not been properly kept, especially as regards married clergy.[2] Over and over again

Their evidence tallies.

these local statutes present identical features ; the same abuses among the clergy, the same reiteration of the enactments, the same reliance on Rome for the impulse and driving force which were needed to produce any reform.

In the year 1240 Walter de Cantelupe drew up a very full set of canons for his diocese of Worcester,

[1] Bliss, i. 85, 105.   [2] Wilkins, *Concilia,* i. 707.

on which we may make the following summary observations :

1. The whole set professes strict adherence to prior rulings, *patrum et predecessorum nostrorum vestigiis inhaerentes.*

2. Several of these canons expressly repeat leading canons of Otto's Council of 1237 (e. g. § 43, on married clerks : ' We enact nothing new, but devote our whole energies to getting the statutes of the Council of London [1] kept ').

3. Many of the others repeat the rules laid down in the canon law.[2]

4. The only articles that can be called peculiarly English touch on very local superstitions, such as holy wells (§ 20), or sports in churchyards (§§ 4, 47), and are of small importance.

5. The general picture exactly bears out the picture drawn in Giraldus's work ; a clergy slack, ignorant, backward, unspiritual even when not actually immoral, greedy of fees (§§ 15, 21, 23, 32, 35–6) ; often illiterate, gamblers, brawlers, professional false witnesses ; in a word, a state of things crying aloud for drastic and continuous action on the part of the central power.

II. The *Gemma Ecclesiastica* of Giraldus Cambrensis was his favourite, his gem ; the one work

Evidence from Giraldus.

---

[1] Evidently *Londonensis*, not *Lugdunensis*, as in Wilkins's text.

[2] Thus numbers 3, 22, 31, 33, 35, 36, 37, 38, 41, and most of the long series of rules for the clergy which follow after 47 correspond to Otto's 3, 5, 18, 8, 4.

which the author assures us Innocent III reserved for his own reading. It primarily applies to the Welsh Church, and that Church, it may be said, was ruder and more backward than the English Church. But on the other hand it was less corrupted in some respects, such as non-residence ; and even in its worse view may be taken as typical of evils which are to be noted in the English Church, if in a lesser degree. The work deals only with the secular clergy, who were as yet far behind the monastic, though two centuries later their state was more wholesome. It is intensely practical ; it deals with actual difficulties that he had seen, and actual cases met often in his own experience, as well as what he had heard from others, and what he had read for himself.

State of popular beliefs. It is highly characteristic of the time that the main topic, the centre of faith and discipline, is the Mass ; twenty-one out of fifty-four chapters of the first half of the book are on this subject. On such a topic the popular mind was ready to run into a wild thaumaturgy which, as extremes meet, amounts to the grossest materialism.[1] Certainly it required a central oracle to keep things both uniform and sane, especially seeing that the mode of transubstantiation was not yet necessarily

---

[1] e.g. Giraldus, *Gemma Eccl.*, p. 39. The Eucharist changing into a hand of flesh to rebuke the woman who had made the wafers.

defined,[1] though later it came to be so. The belief in demonic possession, and the grotesque interpositions of devils, are among the chief things which repel a reader of mediaeval religious books. The evil spirit that possessed the young lady who thrice slapped a holy man on the face, the devil who took advantage of a hasty husband's malediction, these for us have come to have an almost burlesque flavour.

But such stories and beliefs are an expression of the intense reality of the time. Not without reason do these spirits take the name and form of the old heathen deities. The battle between the new Christianity and the old barbarism was but half won. The savagery of the Teutonic world, the corruption of the classic world, jostled at every turn the mysticism and ideal purity of Christianity. The universe was indeed governed by God and His angels : they were all about us. But the Devil and his angels were as real and as omnipresent too. As every virtue was embodied in some spirit, so every sin took the concrete form of some diabolical obsession. In one remarkable passage Giraldus [2] shows us that some of the finer minds were beginning to revolt from this materialization of sin, or at least from undue dwelling on it. At the same time he justly feels that it expresses a reality to the popular conscience, and that it

[1] p. 28. *Non erubescendum ignorare fateri.*
[2] p. 64, ll. 1-4.

must be met on its own ground. And while thus
meeting the popular view and making terms with
it, the mediaeval Church did not, as is vulgarly
believed, increase and exaggerate the current
superstition, that gross spiritualism which often
comes so near the fashionable spiritualism of our
own day. The Church was responsible neither for
its creation, nor for its encouragement. What
she did was, on the whole, to tone it down, to pare
away its chief feature, the element of uncontrol-
lableness ; to bring this world of terrors [1] within
rule and measure ; to make the achievement of
victory over it a plain matter of business, a thing
to be done by hard prayer, penance, and good
works. Hence, with all his formidable ubiquity
and cunning, there is a touch of the contemptible,
even of the ludicrous, about the mediaeval Devil.
He is always getting cheated in his bargains,[2]
sometimes very unfairly cheated ; and he always
gets the worst of it when he encounters a saint.
He is even rather slow to realize his own limitations ; for example, the fact that he only lost
by entering the bodies of the excommunicated;[3]
and rarely has he such a triumph as he has in the
story of Galiena,[4] as told by Baldwin, Archbishop
of Canterbury, while he was Bishop of Worcester.

Of simony Giraldus gives many examples ; the
bishop who bet an applicant a hundred marks

*Influ-
ence of
the
Church.*

*Need of
central
disci-
pline.*

---

[1] Giraldus, p. 98.   [2] p. 75, end.
[3] p. 159.   [4] pp. 228–30.

that he would get a certain prebend ;[1] another
who said, ' Why should I give my preferments to
those who have given nothing for them ? ' ; another
who maintained that small livings should go by
merit, but fat ones to his relations ; the bishop
who exacted the two hundred sheep, when the
recipient had only meant to promise two hundred
eggs (ova).[2] He quotes Alexander III's saying : [3]
' When God deprived bishops of sons, the devil
gave them nephews ; ' and he thinks that things
will remain thus, unless prelates are saints like
Thomas of Canterbury, or without family like
Melchisedec.[4] Celibacy he regards as an unattain-
able aim. He points out that it was not ordered
in the Gospels or by the Apostles, but only introduced in the West for the sake of decorum and
purity ; but now it has broken down. He therefore approves the movement [5] to enforce it in
higher orders only, a result which he declares
Alexander III had nearly achieved. As things
are, concubinage in the clergy is perfectly common,[6]
and is the root cause of all their abuses.[7]

Besides their simony, the offences of the prelates
are so many that they require dividing [8] under
headings ; indeed, one might make a library [9] of
the enormities of these *miseri moderni temporis
episcopi*, who are fishers of money, not fishers of
men ; who sell justice, traffic in pardons, visit

[1] p. 295.   [2] p. 332.   [3] p. 304.   [4] p. 296.   [5] ii, c. v.
[6] part ii, p. 277.   [7] p. 281.   [8] part ii, p. 293.   [9] part ii, p. 294.

their dioceses not once in seven years ; and who,
even if they do well at first, yet soon become
corrupt.[1] What bishop is a true pastor ? Is there
one who has got in without the aid of court
favour ? ' I do not say bishops cannot be saved,
but I do say it is in our days harder for them than
for other men.'

Another charge which the clergy as a whole
undoubtedly deserved was the charge of ignorance.
Examples of this ignorance are many ; there is
the bishop who fined a priest for having joined
the sect of Catholics ; [2] the priest who confused
Barnabas with Barabbas, and St. Jude with Judas ;
the other who translated *Iohannes ante portam
Latinam* as ' John who, leading the way, carried
Latin into England ' ; a third who preached on
our Lord using hyssop (*Dominus his opus habet*) ;
a fourth who discovered a king called Busillis
(*in die-bus illis*) ; and the archbishop who first
tried *in isto sacro synodo*, then being prompted
with an *a*, tried *in ista sacra synoda*, then hearing
his prompter say *o* and *a* tried *in isto sacro synoda*.
Giraldus has pages of these stories,[3] and attributes
some of the evil to the displacement of the study
of literature by the study of law, a change which
it seems the Sibyl had foretold.

Abuses
of cleri-
cal offi-
cials.

A very curious chapter [4] shows the tyranny
which was exercised over the clergy in especial

[1] pp. 294–304.   [2] p. 331.
[3] pp. 341–9.   [4] Book ii, chap. 32.

by the new functionaries, the bishops' *officiales*. A good prelate often had an official so bad that it was like the case of the monsters who had maidens' faces and harpies' bodies. These officials were three : the bishop's confessor, who exercised his cure of souls, his steward, and the archdeacon who did his judicial work. They were chosen for fiscal, not spiritual qualities ; in fact the offices were put up to sale. The reputation of the bishop's steward may be gathered from the story of the blaspheming gambler, who offered his last coins to any one who would show him how to avenge himself on Providence ; the prize was awarded to a bystander who said, ' Become a bishop's steward.' The reputation of the arch- deacon had ' made his name almost equal to that of archdevil '. He will not allow parties in a suit to compromise till his palm is well greased. He turns the canonical rules about affinity into an engine for breaking or making marriages at a price. Worse than himself is the gang of needy relatives and hangers-on who follow him. The whole class are cormorants, ravens, birds of prey, flies spoiling the ointment, unclean dogs who hunt the game into the nets for their masters. They are fond of saying, ' The labourer is worthy of his hire ; ' but what about the labourer's rabble of atten- dants, including huntsmen and falconers ? They make the lesser clergy take oath that they will send all cases up to the bishop's court, though

Pope Alexander forbade such oaths. In fact
it is mainly their fault that the whole body of
the Church is infected through and through with
this sin of avarice ; from the sole of the foot
to the crown of the head there is no soundness
in it.

Abuses among ordinary clergy. Despite all the orders of Councils, money was
still taken for the several sacraments, baptism,
matrimony, extreme unction, and ordination,[1] as
well as for funerals, institutions, consecrations,
anniversaries, and for absolution.[2] It was impossible to prevent money passing on these
occasions, and practically impossible to keep a
clear line between gratuities and fees, between
payment on these occasions and payment for
these objects, between money penalties for sins
and money consideration for absolution.[3] But
there is not much disguise of the pecuniary motive
in the case of the priest who took every mass as
far as the offertory, and then began a new mass ;
or the subdeacon, who being unqualified to read
the Gospel, read two epistles instead, and pocketed
the alms and oblations with the remark that two
epistles were equal to one Gospel any day ;[4] or
the ministers who multiplied masses, anniversaries,
and monthly obits, or made a bid for a big collection by inventing new masses, as for those slain
around Jerusalem, for instance.[5] We hear also

[1] pp. 46, 281.   [2] p. 312.   [3] ii. 32, end.
[4] p. 128.   [5] p. 135.

of the Eucharist being perverted to the purpose
of magic ; for example, there is the man who says
masses over the waxen image of his enemy, or
repeats a great number of masses for the dead
always coupled with an enemy's name. And there
are frequent warnings against the revelling and
drinking bouts in which clergy and laity, men and
women, met together with scandalous consequences.[1]

A writer conscious of all these evils in the The cen-
Church would naturally look to the Holy See as power.
an ally. Giraldus tells the story of Simon of
Tournay, who was stricken with paralysis of the
tongue for having said petulantly, when he could
not get an immediate audience of the Pope,
' One can only get at Simon Peter through Simon
Magus.' He sees how the power of excommunication was abused for local purposes by prelates
who pronounced it lightly, frequently, and without
consideration ; [2] hence in England, where it was
once so dreaded, it was now held in more contempt
than in any other country. This local abuse
needed control from the centre. But Giraldus is
not ultra-Papalist. The power to bind and loose
is in his eyes a declaratory power, like that of the
priest to whom the leper showed himself.[3] ' He
who hath not deserved the sentence of the Church
is not hurt by it, unless he show contempt of it.'
Here he is following the French school, from whose

[1] pp. 258, 261.   [2] pp. 159–60.   [3] pp. 48–50.

great master, Peter Lombard, he borrows largely on this topic.

III. Our next documentary source is the Burton Annals, in which are given two pieces of evidence, the Coventry visitation, and the Berkshire rectors' protest.

The Burton annalist expressly states what indeed is self-evident, that the articles of visitation in Coventry and Lichfield are derived from the articles of Grosseteste's visitation, made in 1238 (or 1237). This shows that Grosseteste's articles were not regarded as exceptional or unwarranted. We know too that Robert de Weseham, Dean of Lincoln, was made Bishop of Coventry in 1244, as a part of Grosseteste's settlement with the Chapter.[1] The Burton articles, moreover, like their exemplar, support the evidence given in Otto's legatine constitutions of 1237, not merely as to the grossness of the evils, but also as to their wide prevalence. It is the same picture of a debased clergy ; often married, given to taverns and brawling, trading and usury ; embezzling the money for lights and for chrismalia, and grasping at obits. Many churches too are held by simony, farmed out to laymen, robbed of their tithes, and used for markets and festivals and law courts. Only two articles refer to the laity ; but as these imply that witchcraft and

[1] *Ann. Burt.* 267.

adultery were regarded as common, we cannot be very optimistic about lay conditions.

If the test of Grosseteste's letters is also applied to the charges brought by the Legate in 1237, the answer is the same ; whether they are grave charges, like the use of the Eucharist and other sacraments as means to extort money, or the prevalence of non-residence ; or technical charges, as the non-dedication of churches. It is sufficiently significant that the first article of all is ' *de vita archidiaconi et familiae eius*', and that four separate articles of the thirty-five are on sexual immorality of the clergy.

Evidence of Grosseteste's letters.

IV. The Berkshire rectors' famous protest, given in Matthew Paris [1] as belonging to 1240, is in the Burton Annals dated 1244, and ascribed to the whole body of English rectors. But the Burton annalist is apt to misplace his documents ; thus he ascribes Innocent's letter of 1253 to 1258, and he confuses the occasion of Innocent's demands in 1244 with the earlier occasion of Gregory IX's demand for one-fifth of clerical revenues in 1240. The circumstances as well as the wording of the protest obviously apply to 1240, not to 1244 ; among such circumstantial details are the reference to Frederick's position, and to his blockading the roads ; the fear of a second precedent setting up a custom ; the fact that the Legate was trying to deal with small clerical assemblies, because

The Berkshire Rectors' protest.

[1] iv. 38 ; *Ann. Monast.* (Burton) i. 265.

he had failed at Northampton to move the bishops, who said that the country clergy must be consulted. Moreover, on the other hand, the protest contains no reference to the particular circumstances of 1244, when Master Martin was dealing specially with the prelates. We have good reason to believe that the Burton annalist did not get hold of the document till years after; for we find that Matthew Paris could only insert it on a fly-leaf—that is, it only reached him at some time subsequent to its date. These subsequent documents he took great pains to date accurately; and the excellence of his information about this particular document is shown by his version of it, which contains more clauses than the version in the Burton Annals, and gives far better readings in many places.

Now if the grounds of the protest be examined, it will be seen that there is no attack on the theory of Papal omnipotence. The nearest approach to such an attack is in § 3. Of the others, § 1 argues that there is no obligation for the clergy to join in an attack on the Emperor for his occupation of the Papal States, because that act is not heresy, and only against heresy is the secular arm invoked. The Emperor has not been condemned by judgement of the Church as a heretic, nor is he to be treated as an excommunicate, since he offers to abide by the voice of a council. § 2 says that the patrimony of prelates is their own, much as the Pope's is his own. In §§ 3, 4, ' Whatsoever thou shalt bind or loose upon earth ' is the text, not ' Whatsoever thou shalt grasp or exact '. Our Lord retains the supremacy, though he gave St. Peter the adminis-tration ; so the separate churches are under the Pope's care, but not under his ownership.

The remaining paragraphs run as follows :

§ 5. Church revenues are for the ministers and the poor, and cannot be diverted.

§ 6. The clergy even now have slender revenues, and often there are bad harvests and dearths ; they cannot see the poor starve before their eyes ; yet no English clerk is now allowed to hold more than one benefice without special dispensation.

§ 7. On the last occasion of such a contribution, it was wasted because the Pope and the Emperor at once made a collusive treaty (1229). A second contribution would be dangerous, for the law has a maxim, ' An act repeated makes a custom.'

§ 8. The Emperor would seize and slay those who contributed against him, whenever they should have occasion to repair to the Holy See ; and his power would be a peril to England.

§ 9. Such a contribution could not be made without the consent of the King and magnates as patrons.

§ 10. The King is the Emperor's ally, and would have to be consulted.

§ 11. The present Pope on the last occasion promised that it should not be made a precedent ;

and to consent would be to put the English clergy below those of any other nation, for the French clergy have already refused to contribute.

§ 12. Most of the clergy, having already taken vows of Crusade, cannot discharge these vows in addition to this payment; also they claim the three years' protection of their estates allowed to men under such vows.

Its nega-tive evi-dence. These clauses present the Berkshire rectors in various lights, as caustic critics of the past, as champions of the rights of patrons and of the poor, as acute debaters of scriptural and legal texts. But the whole protest added together does not make them Protestants. They pass by the crucial matter, the theory of Papal supremacy; the question whether it is to be *dominium* or only *cura* is a point often raised in these struggles, but a point with no reality in it. What is *dominium*? Is it mastery, ownership? or is it rule, sovereignty? Where does ' administration ' end and ' appro-priation ' begin? If the Pope is Peter, if he is the rock on which the Church is built, then he is *Pleni-tudo po-testatis* of the Pope. supreme, and holds the *plenitudo potestatis*. His power may be tyrannically used, and the tyranny may be pointed out, even with telling personal allusions; it may even be evaded on ingenious if mutually destructive pleas. But it cannot be denied; it is the Rock. ' That everything in the world is subject to the Roman pontiff, is an article of faith necessary to salvation.' Boniface VIII was not the first to say this. The very completeness of the acceptance allows a certain laxity of practice, and tolerates outspoken criticism ; just as we Englishmen tolerate and even join in criticism of our own country, because we have a quiet assurance that when all possible concessions have been made to other nationalities, the verdict still must be, England first, the rest nowhere.

What chiefly strikes a modern reader is the outspokenness of the Berkshire criticisms, and the almost ferocious determination in Berkshire to avoid payment. But both things are familiar to any one conversant with mediaeval documents. The really striking things are : first, that the criticism is only criticism, and does not approach to mutiny ; in fact, it starts from the unexpressed axiom that mutiny is inconceivable ; secondly, that the Papacy paid so little heed to all this, and took for granted that payment would be made in the end. It negotiated the amount in France as a bill drawn on a sluggish but perfectly solvent debtor, and the Berkshire recalcitrants had to end by paying up.

V. We have seen that our Legate in 1237 had drastic views as to the reforms needed for the Church in England. When we tested these views by collating them with those of Giraldus, Grosse-teste, and the Burton annalist, we were citing witnesses who at least lived at the time. To set

Evidence from John Athon, J. de Burgh, and Lyndwood.

beside theirs the testimony of John Athon might seem something of an anachronism. For though he is our earliest writer on ' English ' Canon Law, though he expressly wrote a commentary on the legatine constitutions of Otto, though he was himself a Church dignitary, an old pupil of Archbishop Stratford, and an Oxford man, still with all these merits it must be admitted that he wrote not much less than a century after his text. Yet, despite this interval of time, he may be utilized as a witness to the continuous importance of the Papal supremacy over the English Church, and that because of certain considerations. In the first place, the view he expresses is clearly one which represents a continuous tradition. It is the view expressed in the *Pupilla Oculi* of John de Burgh (1385), and by William Lyndwood (1430). All three are most competent to speak. Lyndwood was ' official ' to Archbishop Chichele in 1430, and a very learned man, though he wrote for ordinary students. De Burgh was Chancellor of Cambridge, and had written a fuller *Sacerdotis Oculus*, of which the *Pupilla Oculi* is a condensed manual for priests. Athon had written learned and critical work before he wrote this commentary for the public—a very ignorant public certainly, for it had to have the ablative absolute explained to it, and to be informed that *tempus* means ' time ', not ' weather '. In the second place, John Athon himself regards his work merely as a continuation of the standard glossators, a sort of elements of Canon Law *in usum Delphini* for English ecclesiastical courts, an edition with a commentary and glossary of the two texts which were most used in England, the legatine constitutions of Otto and Ottobono. He evidently regards his commentary as the first written in England upon these legatine constitutions. There is no precedent of English authority to which he can refer. All his citations are from the classical canonist authorities : John Andreae (ob. 1348), the greatest of all canonists ; John le Moine (ob. 1313) ; the Archdeacon Guy de Baysis, author of the *Rosary* ; William Durand, author of the *Speculum* and the chief authority on procedure ; Pope Innocent IV ; and Hostiensis, that is, the Cardinal Henry of Susa, Bishop of Ostia.

The third of these considerations is, that the influences during the period 1250–1330 were such that it is a euphemism to describe them merely as unfavourable to any increase of Papalism in England. The Holy See had lately been transferred to Avignon, a transference which men soon came to regard as one from Rome to Babylon. France was becoming the hereditary national foe, and the Papacy had deteriorated into an unconscionable tool of French policy. The amount and kind of English Papalism may therefore safely be reckoned as having been at least as great in the middle of the thirteenth century as the

amount and kind which is found surviving about
the middle of the fourteenth century. The
Papalism set forth in this work, dated about 1336,
is all the more convincing because of a curious
undertone of reluctance about it. The Pope of
these days, so Athon feels, is an extortioner and
a jobber, and worse still, he is a Frenchman.
Still, he is the Pope ; and the Pope must be
admitted to wield vast powers of general supremacy, of judicature and of dispensation ; thus
English Councils are held by the authority of the
Pope.[1] This authority is deputed to Legates
a latere, who can therefore call a council even in
the harvest season,[2] despite bishops' protests.
The Pope cannot err once he is really informed.[3]
There are many cases which the Pope alone can
judge,[4] and many where he alone can give a dispensation, especially in homicide and simony.[5]
He stands above all patriarchs and primates. His
dispensations may be misplaced and inexpedient,
they may be mere *dissipationes*, but there they
are : *non tamen ignoro Papam sic posse dispensare.*
He has the power, howsoever he may use it.

The whole of John Athon's commentary is also
an unhesitating admission of the abuses found in
the Church of England at the legatine inquest of
1237. He never traverses the indictment, never
protests against its severity, but adds touches and
piquancies of his own.

[1] p. 1 k.   [2] p. 5 c.   [3] p. 10 p.   [4] p. 41 d.   [5] p. 55.

' Our prelates are pilots asleep in the storm.'
' The clergy uncanonically wear long beards :
I would have them shorn to their very gums.' [1]
' Churchmen strain the canons by casuistry, so
as to give countenance to England's greatest
evil, robbers.' [2]   ' The rural deans have neither
the courage nor the knowledge for their work.'
' They are fat with the plunder and the blood of
the poor.' [3]   ' The northern province does not
conform to the rules of the southern.' [4]   ' Forgers
of the King's seal are often found to be clerks :
such offenders are justly branded, whether clerks
or not.' [5]   ' The conduct of the *officiales* suggests
either the derivation from *officio*, to do hurt ; or
else, if derived from *officium*, duty, it is on the
lucus a non lucendo principle, but it is hard to
say whether it be their own iniquity, or at the
instigation of hypocritical superiors.' [6]   ' Ecclesiastical lawyers say to a scrupulous client, Answer
thus and you will lose your case ; but they fail
to add, if you do not answer thus, you will lose
your soul.'   A long list of such excerpts might
be made, but these suffice to show that the native
churchman took an even gloomier view of the
English Church than the Roman Legate had done.

VI. The opening of the Papal archives by
Leo XIII gave access to an immense body of
confidential documents hitherto known only by

[1] p. 37.   [2] pp. 48–50.   [3] p. 61 i.
[4] p. 65 2.   [5] p. 69 l.   [6] p. 68 l.

a few excerpts, such as Pertz's in 1824. The
Registers which cover the years 1216 to 1307 are
in twenty-three volumes ; the documents therein
which came from Innocent IV numbeɪ 8,352.
Most of them are documents issued to the clergy.
They supply a vast mass of evidence to test the
conclusions as to the mediaeval Church which
are drawn from other sources. Their historic
value depends on the following characteristics :

1. They are authentic, for they are registrations
of the actual minutes or drafts out of which were
drawn up the deeds as finally issued ; or, in a few
cases, particularly where the registration is belated
or where the draft had got mislaid, they are copies
of the original deeds.

2. They are not second-hand excerpts from
a larger original Register.[1]

3. They are contemporaneous with the original
deeds. The date is, in cases of ' common form ',
the day on which the grant was approved by the
Pope ; or in the case of the *legenda*—that is, those
which were read over to the Pope for his final
approval—the date when that approval was given.
Hence very often the date in the Register is more
trustworthy than the date in the deed itself, which
it might have been found expedient to antedate
or to postdate. The belated entries, often several
months late, are generally due to a deed having

[1] Pertz and Rodenberg in *Epist. Pontif.* i, ii, iii, and *Neues
Archiv*, x. 510–85.

been sent back by the holder for registration afterwards. But as a rule a mass of minutes and rough drafts lay before the scribe, and he exercised a certain sort of grouping in entering them on the Register.

4. They are uncoloured and genuine transcripts. The original motive in forming the Register was to supply the Curia with a store of precedents and reliable references. Their relation to the history of that time is what is called ' undesigned coincidence '. They record deeds which were actually issued, and no others. They were never meant to be seen outside the Curia, and have no ulterior object of influencing outside opinion. In fact, they were as a rule never meant to go out of the custody of the head officials of the Chancery.

Hence (5) they were very carefully drawn up, and their wording was scrupulously faithful to their originals. Registration soon became very popular ; a lost original could be replaced from the registered copy. The rapid development of the system meant also the rise of a highly-trained professional class with many grades, from some cardinal who, as Chancellor, drew up lists of influential persons to whom the important circulars should go out, down to the mere copying clerks, who, however, had to be good Latinists and expert draftsmen. One must not be misled by the various slips, especially those made in the spelling of non-Latin countries. What the Registrar wanted was a record of the exact powers conferred. The name of an official might be reduced to an initial, and a mere shot might be made at the name of a place ; this did not matter. Lonkeincenton[1] for Long Itchington did not affect the essence of a precedent, even if it had already been spelt Lonchiecenton[2] in the same Chancery.

6. The registered deeds were only a part, perhaps not even a very large part, of the total number of deeds issued. Even in Potthast's collection there are some hundreds of deeds of Innocent IV which are not represented in the Registers. But without doubt the part is fairly representative of the whole. For, after all, with the exception of a handful of *litterae Curiales* inserted at the end of each year—that is, deeds registered by official order, as relating to affairs of high policy or as affecting the *familia* of the Pope and cardinals, —with this exception the question of registration or non-registration was a question for the holder. He had to pay, first, the high official who got him the grace, then the abbreviator who drew the minutes, then the reader who got them passed, then the bullator who affixed the leaden seal ; if after all this he had still any money left, he might buy the luxury of registration.

If from all the 8,352 deeds in the Registers of Innocent IV we select those which concern

---

[1] Berger, *Les Registres d'Innocent IV*, 3243.
[2] Ibid. 1533.

England, they fall into three groups. In one group they show (a) the ordinary machinery of Papal administration at the ordinary routine. ordinary machinery of Papal administration at work. In another would come those which illustrate peculiar features in the pontificate of Innocent IV. Of these two groups, however, there will be not a few overlapping cases ; for the peculiarity of Innocent IV's activity lies not so much in the creation of new machinery as in the application of the ordinary machinery in extraordinary ways, and this therefore would constitute the third group of documents. Every Pope since Innocent III had a vast number of elections of prelates brought to him for adjudication, but no Pope turned these so openly into opportunities for buying support in his political campaign as did Innocent IV when, for instance, he used the archbishopric of Canterbury for a sop to Savoy [1] in September 1243, and the bishopric of Winchester to secure Henry III in February 1251.[2]

To take the first group. We see the action of the Papacy in property law from cases of dower and wills ; in marriage law, dispensation as to kinship, dispensation as to illegitimacy for orders or for holding benefices; in suits as to advowsons and tithe ; in exchanges between abbeys or prelates ; in settlements inside chapter bodies, a very common source of strife; in

[1] Ibid. 119.   [2] Ibid. 4911.

strengthening the hands of bishops to set up
vicars. We see it as the only power that can
scrutinize and approve new foundations, or that
can raise a perennial revenue to build or restore
churches, or that can give release from excommunication in serious cases, such as any offence
against a clerk, or when pronounced by a bishop ;
and we must remember that excommunication
can be incurred quite unwittingly.

Papal
dele-
gates. For every case in the Registers there would be
scores of cases decided by local application of
Papal power through Papal delegates, who would
often be foreigners beneficed in England.[1] But
often also these delegates would be English
prelates holding permanent Papal commissions,
such as the Bishops of Lincoln and Worcester
held for years in the business of the Crusade ;
or they would be English delegates appointed
ad hoc in a particular case. Again, for every case
that came before the supreme court, whether
actually at Rome or by delegation in England,
there would be many lesser cases that never got
up so far, but which would be settled in the
bishops' courts by their archdeacons, or even by
the rural deans ; or else they would be satisfied
with appealing from the bishop to the archbishop.

---

[1] As Henry of Susa, the great Hostiensis of the Canonists,
recalled when he became Cardinal Bishop of Ostia ; but he was
in England 1244 (M. Paris, iii. 713) ; or John Saracen, Dean
of Wells, Papal Subdeacon and Chaplain, a very frequent
figure in the Registers (3743, 3772, 4086, &c.).

But for all these lesser and local cases it was the
decision in the central court that set the precedent.

Fortunately the benefit of Papal control could
be obtained without necessarily evoking the cause
to Rome. A threat to do so would often suffice.
For a journey to Rome or even to Lyons was no
light matter, when of three who set out on the
undertaking, one might be taken by pirates, one
turn back after crossing the Channel, and only
one reach his destination.[1] On the other hand, this
distance of the bank of issue made it easier to
forge its notes. Innocent III had issued elaborate
directions how to detect nine different sorts of
sham Papal bulls ; and Innocent IV, in breaking
up a whole gang of reverend forgers who seem to
have had a long as well as a lucrative run, charges
connivance against the prelates.[2]

The monasteries were a part of the English Value of
Church in which Papal control was absolutely Rome to
the
indispensable. They were exposed to all sorts of monks ;
exactions from secular prelates, to claims of tithes,
to vexatious summons, to violent intrusions by
force, to fraudulent alienations by their own
vassals ; from all these evils nothing but the long
arm of Rome could save them. They found it
well to get their charters confirmed,[3] or even
re-drafted, after a fire or other damage.[4]

[1] *Les Registres d'Innocent IV*, 116.   [2] Ibid. 4086.
[3] The Cistercians, 477–81 ; Sempringham, 6364.
[4] Glastonbury, 1341.

The newer orders required constant protection against the jealousies of the rest of the clergy.[1] Often they needed permission to convert some of their church revenues towards the sustenance of their inmates,[2] and particularly in the Order of Sempringham, in which we hear of foundations where there are a hundred or two hundred nuns half-starved. A very common privilege granted is that of leave for the monks to wear caps at service, in consideration of the rigours of the English climate. The right for an abbot to have some episcopal insignia, the mitre, the ring, the sandals, the crosier, and to give an episcopal benediction, was highly valued, and no doubt well paid for.[3]

yet they need control.

On the other side of the account, the monasteries represented a great danger to the Church. A large number of the advowsons had fallen into their hands ; for example, Glastonbury had six in one place, Sempringham had sixty-two in all. In this last case the unusually solemn act of confirmation, sealed and signed by the Pope and seven cardinals, is followed at a short interval by a bull empowering the proctors of the Order to pledge its credit for fifteen hundred marks ' for expenses incurred at the See of Rome ', some

[1] Dominicans, 449–58.

[2] e.g. Malmesbury, 4150; St. Augustine's, Canterbury, Hospitallers, 2463–4.

[3] St. Mary's, York ; Westminster ; Evesham; Coventry; Shrewsbury.

£20,000 in modern money. Advowsons held by abbeys often meant non-residence or ill-paid vicars; it cost Grosseteste a long struggle and a journey to Lyons before he could get even this abuse moderated. The wealth and corporate pride of the monks frequently, as at Canterbury and Bath, led them into incursions into episcopal elections. They resisted any visitation by bishops; and here too Grosseteste had great difficulty in convincing the Curia against powerful bodies which were traditional allies of the Papacy, and which spared no money to support their case. It was not that the monasteries were as yet flagrantly corrupt or immoral, but they were certainly drifting into indolent comfort; they were narrow in their views; they were soon to decline from their learning and culture. The vivid picture of monastic life and thought given in Caesar of Heisterbach's *Dialogus de Miraculis*, despite some features that are beautiful and sincere, has yet much in it that is unspiritual and unnatural, petty, even revolting. It is like the smell of stale incense.

If we take the documents relating to so prominent a churchman as Grosseteste, we get a striking view of the continuity and importance of the Papal influence. Besides the bulls ratifying his plans for endowment of vicarages and for correction of monastic discipline, there are others evoking to the Curia and settling on appeal the long contest between himself and the Chapter; *Evidence from Bulls issued to Grosseteste.*

appointing him on a commission to inquire into
the claims of Edmund Rich to canonization ;
protecting him from any excommunication save
by special mandate, or from summons outside his
diocese, or from Papal commission ; authorizing
him to take steps against men who have deserted
their wives to become monks, and to give leave
of absence to study theology at the University ;
allowing three of his clerks to hold an extra benefice
each ; absolving him from excommunication incurred unwittingly ; ordering him to uphold the
rights of two Papal provisors ; putting in his
hand coercive power against rectors who act as
justices, sheriffs, or bailiffs ; empowering him to
raise to priests' orders five clerks, though dis-
qualified by illegitimate birth. There are also
a great number of orders to him as Papal commissioner for the Crusade ; to pay £1,000 to
William Longsword ; to respect the Templars'
immunities ; to distribute to active Crusaders the
legacies and commutations of vows ; to satisfy
Henry III without paying these moneys to him ;
to sanction a new code of rules for Holy Cross
Priory. This is the picture of a central power
alert, active, implicitly obeyed, exercising an
authority which for the most part is obviously
both centripetal and salutary. At last, in October
1250, he was released from the office, subject to
audit of his accounts.

In the second group of the documents in this

Register come those which illustrate peculiarities
of Innocent IV's pontificate. Grants of benefices
to Papal nephews, Papal subdeacons and chaplains, writers of the Papal Chancery, and to
nominees of cardinals, are almost innumerable.
A typical case is the general licence to hold in
plurality several benefices, even with the cure of
souls, a licence issued to Ottobono, ' our nephew
and chaplain ', who was already, as it happened,
Chancellor of Reims and Archdeacon of Parma,
and to his three nephews, Percival, Frederick, and
Giles, all of whom held French canonries already.
Besides these cases, a great number of provisions
are issued to foreigners, who as creditors or otherwise had some claim on the Pope. Thus the Counts
of Vico were important nobles near Rome, and
provision to the extent of thirty or fifty marks
is to be made[1] for a scion of this family. Most
numerous of all are the licences to hold in plurality.
There are a hundred and forty-three such licences
affecting England in the first five years, and in
the last five and a half years, a hundred and fifty-
nine. In a few of these cases some excuses are
assigned : one of the livings is small,[2] or the
applicant is a clerk of some great personage,[3] or
he is of noble birth.[4] In the vast majority there
is no such excuse offered ; and some instances
are very flagrant, such as the following : ' Manuel

[1] 3743.   [2] 16 Kal. Nov. 1250.
[3] 1251, Nov.–Jan.   [4] End of July 1250.

de Sauro, citizen of Genoa, kinsman of the Pope,
to hold the rectory of Kettering and other benefices,
though he is non-resident and not in orders.'
The abuse was accentuated by instructions to
bishops to evict all pluralists who were not
fortified by Papal licence. The abuse of dispensations went to the length of issuing them in
sheaves. In June 1248 the new Bishop of Bath and
Wells was carrying on a brisk traffic at the Curia.[1]
He bought protection from excommunication for
himself and his staff ; leave to celebrate mass
with them during an interdict ; protection from
provisions ; power to evict incumbents who were
absentees or of illegitimate birth, unless they could
show a Papal licence ; and power to admit to
orders forty candidates who were of illegitimate
birth. A former bull which authorized him to
hold on to all his former benefices for an extra
year suggests how he raised funds for these
spiritual luxuries.

Parti-
sanship
under
Innocent
IV.
A third group of documents in the Register is
made up of those in which the Papacy is indeed
doing its normal work, but doing it with a partisan
bias. Such would be the decision of elections to
prelacies, and in the cases of elections in Germany
and Italy the bias is unconcealed. In the English
elections, the question of leanings to the Imperialist or anti-Imperialist side did not arise,
and each election was decided by special circum-

[1] 4001–10.

stances, of which the appointments to Canterbury
in 1243, and to Winchester in 1251, are the most
conspicuous instances.

The Papal Registers, then, already suggest an
interesting distinction. The second and third
class of documents make a very different impression on us from that made by the first : it is the
pathological as contrasted with the normal and
healthy functioning of a great organism.

VII. There is another side of Papal activity The
which hardly comes into the Registers, but which Papacy
as an
was of immense importance in its relation to the appeal
court ;
English Church. This was the work done by the
Papacy as an appeal jurisdiction. Such jurisdiction was inherent in the theory of the Pope as
episcopus episcoporum. But in primitive law the
idea of appeal to a higher court was strange. It was,
therefore, not till after the Norman Conquest had
opened the way for influences derived from
Roman law that the idea of appealing to Rome
developed rapidly. This development over the
whole area of Europe, like the parallel development of feudalism some three centuries earlier,
means that it was a living growth from below,
not a mechanical structure superimposed from
above. For many reasons men thronged to lay
their cases at the blessed feet of the Apostle. The
very theory of Canon Law was that it was an
exposition of the law of God ; it was best, therefore, to go at once to the highest expositor, God's

Vicar on earth. At Rome, too, there would be freedom alike from the local tyranny of prelates and from the local hostility of lay officials. Moreover, the prelates themselves encouraged the practice of appeals. For the law spiritual, in the century between Alexander III and Alexander IV, was in a state of luxuriant and embarrassing growth; and though bishops and archdeacons had to dispense law and justice, they were rarely trained lawyers, or at any rate expert canonists; and of two alternatives, it is far better to pass a case on to a higher court, than to give one's own judgement, only to be overruled on appeal. Moreover, most appeals in Church cases took the form called appeals *a gravamine*—that is, interlocutory appeals before judgement was given, the object being to stay proceedings or even to prevent their inception; and these appeals required no leave of the court at all.

its value to England. The practice of appeal was far more prevalent in England than in any of the leading countries. This was natural, for it must be admitted that England, especially in regard to its Church, was distinctly backward. Then, again, the scheme of Church courts in England was singularly complicated and overlapping. The archbishop had his court of Arches, which was both a court of appeal from the bishops' diocesan jurisdiction, and in virtue of his legatine powers a court of first instance besides. He had his court of

Audience ; his Prerogative court for wills ; his court of Peculiars for his privileged immunities ; his jurisdiction in Convocation ; and an informal personal jurisdiction. The bishop had his consistory court, which included appeals from the archdeacon, and the court of his commissary, which had the right to appeal to the bishop himself. The archdeacons had acquired a customary jurisdiction, independent of the bishops, to a different degree in each diocese. They held chapters of the clergy every five months, and exercised visitation in the bishop's absence. The rural deans prepared articles for the archdeacon's visitation, and made presentment of offenders ; but they were charged with being quite ignorant of canonical rules. All this system, like the feudal hierarchy, needed a strong head, otherwise it spelt anarchy ; and all the more so because of the age-long struggle between Canterbury and York, which makes it hardly an exaggeration to say that there was no one ecclesiastical organization which we can strictly call the Church of England.[1] The choice lay between anarchy and the *plenitudo potestatis*.[2] The struggle between Archbishop Boniface and the bishops of his province shows the sort of thing that might result.

The recourse to Rome was, after all, not a complete departure from native authorities, or a

[1] Maitland, *Canon Law*, p. 114.   [2] Ibid. p. 122.

submission to foreign judges. In the vast majority of cases appeals would be handed over by the Pope to delegates *ad hoc* in England. It was quite common for an applicant to the Curia to suggest names that would be agreeable ; one could thus practically appoint one's own judges, subject only to their being challenged if they were obviously unfair.[1] Besides, the Papal delegates had very elastic powers, to fill up their numbers, to appoint sub-delegates, and to compel service.[2]

Resort to Rome for advice.

Finally, Papal jurisdiction grew very largely out of a need which meets the English student at the very threshold of our history, the need of recourse to Rome for advice and interpretation, such as Gregory the Great gave to Augustine. A modern judge will decline to answer hypothetical cases. But the Holy Father was much more than a judge. He was the counsellor of the faithful, the exponent and interpreter of the oracles of God. To act on his declaration was to be beyond the power of question by rival litigants in this world, or by demon inquisitors in the world to come. This declaratory function was in the fullest activity in the interval between the Decretum of Gratian and the Decretalia of Gregory IX, and again between these Decretals and the supplementary Decretals of Boniface VIII, the Sext. A great

[1] *Hostiensis Summa*, col. 308, ed. Venet. 1605.
[2] 28 X, l. 29.

proportion of the Decretals [1] are, in fact, the answers to questions propounded in this way by anxious prelates, and English prelates seem to have been the most anxious of all. [2]

The Papacy is thus much more than an ordinary court of appeal. In fact, as early as the middle of the thirteenth century, it has come to be the ' universal ordinary '. From the civil law was borrowed the maxim *Roma est patria omnium*, and translated into Church terms this became *Papa est iudex ordinarius omnium*. In other words, a great number of ecclesiastical cases began before Papal delegates. These would be English clerics, but they would be acting under powers and instructions from Rome. Both Bracton [3] and William of Drogheda [4] assume that this is so : that an action in these courts naturally starts with an original *rescriptum domini Papae*. This apparently was more the practice in England than in other countries. [5] What proportion did these cases bear to the whole ? We cannot tell without records of the proceedings in English ecclesiastical courts, and where are these records to be found ? When they are found they should throw light on some subjects of great interest, one, amongst others, the debt

The Pope as ' universal ordinary '.

[1] Lyndwood (p. 272) defines a decretal as a Papal answer to consultation.

[2] Potthast, 2350.   [3] f. 412 ; f. 253 [b].

[4] Maitland, *Canon Law*, 112.

[5] For Italy, cf. Maitland, ibid. p. 113, note ; for France, Fournier, *Les Officialités au moyen âge*.

that the English Church and the English nation owed to the jurisprudence of Papal Rome.

It is peculiarly difficult so to place ourselves as to get an impartial view of the relation of Rome to England in the Middle Ages. It is also notoriously difficult to appreciate the influence of law upon social progress ; for the historian hardly ever does justice to legal conceptions, and the lawyer is apt to be impenitently unhistorical. But when the question on hand is the place of Roman Canon Law in the English Church and State of the thirteenth century, these two difficulties are augmented by others. For besides these two time-honoured and avowed prejudices against the dominance of Rome and the dominance of law, the word Canon Law evokes other prejudices which are just as powerful, if more obscure. It seems to call up associations of a judicature which made every sin feasible, of a penitential system which commuted every offence for money. Then, again, the English mind always likes to keep its abstract ideas in separate bottles, to label religion as for Sundays, and mark it off thus from law, the everyday instrument. Hybrids are regarded with suspicion in general, and a hybrid between law and religion is not likely to satisfy the kindred on either side. Finally, the Canon Law has come in for some hard words at the hands of those who have championed the State against sacerdotalism, from the ' majestic lord who broke the bonds of Rome ', to Thomas Hobbes in whose mind 'spiritual and temporal were two words brought into the world to make men see double ', and who incessantly adduces the text, ' My kingdom is not of this world.'

But to judge the ideal aimed at in the Canon Law by the condition to which its practice had sunk when the world had lost belief in it, is as unhistorical as it would be to judge the monastic ideal by the state of the abbeys in 1536, when the *malleus monachorum* took them in hand. The ideal of the golden age of the canonists was to make a working reality of the kingdom of God upon earth ; to express the laws of that kingdom in a coherent, all-embracing code, and to enforce that code upon the still half-heathen kingdoms of the world. An ideal truly, and predestined to fail ; but a noble ideal.

The aim of Canon Law.

That the clerk hindered from holy orders by a blemish in his birth, that the layman who laid sacrilegious hands upon a clerk, must present himself at the threshold of the Apostles to get absolution, was an outward and visible sign of the inward and spiritual unity of Christendom under its visible head. The General Councils of the Church, the Legates *a latere*, the interposition of commissioners from Rome into the ecclesiastical courts of every land, were further developments of this principle. That it led to vast abuses, to a perversion of the loftiest belief for the most corrupt and tyrannical ends, is a commonplace of history. *Corruptio optimi pessima.* But to confuse the last state with the first, to deny that what came to be so bad was ever good in intent and idea, this is not historical. Whether such a corruption was not inherent and inevitable in the attempt to work a superhuman system by fallible human instruments, whether it is not inherent in the very design of thus cutting up religion into a thing of books and chapters and sections, of precedents and commentaries, may well be asked. But these are questions for others to answer. *Non nostri est tantas componere lites.*

The confessional.
VIII. At the Lateran Council of 1215, Innocent III promulgated a momentous order.[1] Every Christian man or woman was to confess at least once in the year all his sins privily to his own priest, and zealously in his own person perform the penance enjoined on him ; otherwise to be debarred from entry into the Church and from Christian burial. This rule was carried out by the very weighty guarantee that any one who neglected it was presumptively chargeable with heresy.

its results ;
The later results of this rule were somewhat surprising. In the first place, it gave a much greater efficacy to excommunication, which was now backed up by a real executive officer, the confessor, instead of being left to the uncovenanted discretion of a sheriff. Sins tended to be brought

[1] c. 12 X. v. 38.

to a level when they were thus regarded prima facie from the standard of obedience to an ecclesiastical authority. Till they have made their submission to the priest, the parricide and the borrower of books from a library are alike relegated to outer darkness. The first half of Christian duty becomes obedience to the hierarchy, and men are apt to relax when half their duty is done.

In the second place, the confessional implied penance, and penances needed to be classified and tabulated, with the consequence that their externality became more and more prominent, to the neglect of their inner significance. The outward act, often a trivial penalty such as bread and water one day a week, or often a mere money payment, came to be regarded as everything ; and the true and lively faith, without which good works are but filthy rags, had to be reasserted, even with over-emphasis. Here, again, is the nemesis awaiting attempts to stereotype religion into a cut-and-dried set of rules. Thus the passionate impulse of the Middle Ages to realize its ideals and to embody them in a material form ended in a vast system of indulgence and an undisguised tariff of sins.

In the third place, the Church shifted its practical aim. In the earlier centuries she had aimed at permeating European society with Christianity, or at least with her view of Christianity ; at interpenetrating society, law, and even politics,

as well as art and literature, with the principles
of religion. Commerce itself was to be moralized—
a somewhat chimerical aim. But from the middle
of the thirteenth century the aim was less religious
than hierarchical ; it implied the domination of
Church over State, and of clergy over laity, the
demonstration of the civil power's derivation from
ecclesiastical, even the substitution of Church law
for secular. The struggle for the dominance of one
privileged class is accompanied by very unevan-
gelical concessions to the other privileged class.
The Church lets nobles have private baptisms,
marry within prohibited degrees, hold benefices in
plurality and in absence ; while the villein is to be
debarred from orders, and the stain of villeinage is
argued to be a just reason for dissolution of the
marriage tie.

In the fourth place, the spiritual jurisdiction no
doubt lent itself to casuistry, that dark shadow
which has clung closely to all great religious movements, even movements differing so widely as the
Friars, the Jesuits, and the Puritans. This tendency received a sudden impetus from Innocent's
orders for universal confession. The confessional
represented the *forum internum*, and thus came
into collision not only with the law of the State,
but sometimes even with the official law of the
Church. A conflict of this kind was not unknown.
A *Summa Quaestionum*, a book of problems more
than thirty years before the Lateran Council, had

put the case of a man bound to adhere to a wife whom he knows to be not really his wife. ' Yet he sins not if he is obeying a command of the Church. . . . If the objection be raised that he is acting against his conscience and therefore sins, we answer he must let conscience go.' But now, such conflicts necessarily became more frequent. To meet them, a demand arose for manuals of cases for the use of priests : and casuistry is come. But we must not antedate it ; for example, there is very little in John Athon's scheme. It is an attempt on the part of the clergy to win back from the individual what they had lost to the State ; and its spring-time is the fourteenth century, as we can see from Wiclif's denunciations of it as novel.

Yet Innocent III's rule of universal private confession had been directed against definite and grave evils. The ancient scheme of public penance before the congregation had broken down. It had from the first been tainted with two influences derived from Teutonic law, the influence of the wergild with its money commutations, and the influence of the curious practice of vicarious punishment allowed in the case of magnates. The new rule was an attempt to destroy the vulgar material-ism, which looked on penance as something that mechanically wiped out sins, and to substitute the doctrine that it needed *confessio oris* and *contritio cordis* as well as *satisfactio operis* ; and that the essential prerequisite indeed was contrition, as

its original aim.

being the innermost of these three, the one from which the other two would follow as fruit grows on a tree. If this loftier point of view could have been kept up, penance, as the heartfelt offering of the individual's own conscience, need never have relapsed into its former mechanical position. For some time the Lateran decree did do something to elevate it to this higher plane, and incidentally threw aside as lumber the horrible old penitential books, which give one an awful vision of the Augean stable of a Christendom as yet only half Christian. The Lateran decree also helped to increase the tendency towards centralization, because the number of cases increased in which no one but the Apostle himself could give absolution. It is a remarkable fact that just in these first three decades of the thirteenth century so many diverse influences were converging upon one focus ; the result was to heap upon the Papacy numerous powers, not merely by way of appeal, but by way of first resort. Taxation, law-making, judicature, were not so much ' usurped ' by Innocent III and Gregory IX, as thrust upon them; and the same is true of the Church's supreme disciplinary power.

Tendencies to centralization.

LECTURE II

THE PAPACY AND THE MEDIAEVAL LAW OF MARRIAGE

THAT the Papacy was the greatest of all human Papal influence on Society, institutions is a proposition on which students of history might find it not very difficult to agree. But it would be a much more disputable matter to fix the turning-point and crisis in that institution, to answer the question when and how the Papacy, from being the apostle of religion, the organizer of civilization, the heart and soul of Christendom, began to change into a tyranny, an incubus, and a byword. Before an answer can be given it is essential to consider the Papacy in its earlier phase as a power making for righteousness. This power can be seen in action, not only on the English Church, but also on English social life. But to attempt to include in one field of view the whole area of English social life would be defeating our own objects. We should have to stand back so far, and to move our perspective glass in such wide sweeps that all detail, all precision, would be lost. It remains, then, to choose some one province within this wide area, and fix awhile our eyes upon that. Now there is probably nothing which exerts a especially marriage law. deeper influence upon a community than its marriage law ; for in large measure this shapes

the conditions of property, the social ethics, even
the practical working religion, of the community.
What kind of marriage law, then, was it which
England received from her spiritual mother ?

The
Church
and the
law of
marri-
age. To a superficial view, never does the mediaeval
Church stand out in so unpleasing a light as in the
history of her dealings with the marriage laws.

She started, it might be said, with a repulsively
low view of the subject ; she shifted her ground
completely on more than one point ; she left the
laws on it chaotic even beyond mediaeval tolerance
of chaos ; she laid down one principle after another,
only to let lawyers drive a coach-and-six through
each ; she failed to enforce on the State her inter-
pretations, though it had been made her sole
province ; she left many crying scandals and
abuses untouched ; she introduced a dialectical
distinction between *verba de praesenti* and *verba de
futuro* which was a premium on perjury ; she
bound on men's backs the grievous burden of
degrees of consanguinity and affinity ; she carried
these disqualifications to extremes by the fanciful
analogies of *cognatio spiritualis* and *affinitas illegitima* ; and she reserved a power of dispensation so
wide that the rule seemed to become like a rule in
English grammar, all exceptions.

All this is true, but it is not the whole truth; and
the mediaeval Church might say like Themistocles,
' Strike, but hear me.' She has a right to a hearing
even from persons born with minds made up

against her, which might almost be said to be the case with English persons. And even so, it would be a mistake to blame the Church, too hastily, for all the abuses. She had to work upon an extraordinarily complicated and barbarous mass of social customs ; she had to work gradually and tentatively ; she had to work with an eye to Roman law on the one hand, and growing feudal law on the other ; and what two systems of law could be more inharmonious ? Above all she had The texts. to work within the strict limits of certain scriptural examples and maxims which were very narrowly interpreted ; ' It is better to marry than to burn,' ' In the Kingdom of Heaven there is no marrying or giving in marriage,' ' Whom God hath joined, let not man put asunder,' ' The head of the woman is the man,' ' It is good for a man not to marry,'— such are the texts constantly appealed to, while the one authoritative example that was to be made the type and test of a perfect marriage was that of Joseph and Mary.

All this meant that it was only by a long historical process that the Church could get complete control of marriage. The barbarian races had to be converted first ; the temporal power had to cease to make laws for the whole of Christendom ; the see of Rome had to feel itself driven step by step to take up this law-making function. Thus it is that the Church's control cannot be recognized further back than the later ninth

century, the age of Hincmar ; and it cannot be
said to be at its height for much more than the
150 years from Gratian to Boniface VIII, the
golden age of the canon law. At its height it
claimed not only matrimonial causes proper, but
also the allied matters, such as dower, legitimacy,
inheritance. But these excursions into debatable
territory brought it into collision in England
particularly with the lay lawyers, who insisted on
their own rules of dower, their own tests of
legitimacy and inheritance. These collisions were
in the fourteenth and fifteenth centuries. In the
sixteenth came the Reformation.

Yet the Reformation did not make such a difference as is often supposed, and the English marriage
law remained largely canonical and was even
administered by ecclesiastical judges as late as
1867.

The
chaos.

There can be no greater social evil than uncertainty in the marriage law, and excessive
facility of divorce. If this were the United States
of America, with their thirty-seven different laws
of marriage, it might be necessary to bring evidence
for such a proposition. But in this less advanced
country the proposition may perhaps be allowed
as axiomatic. Now the varying standards of what
constituted a valid marriage in the early Middle
Ages would almost defy enumeration. Into this
chaos the Church had to bring some degree of
unity and rational principle. No wonder that her

action was cautious, even timid. She had to take account of Jewish tradition and ceremonial observances ; of Roman law and the different types of marriage therein allowed ; and of the tenacious Germanic customs varying in each tribal area.

The Hebrew tradition laid a disastrous stress on the physical side ; Roman law laid its chief weight on consensus ; the Teutonic tribes contributed the elements of betrothal, dower, and the mund. Outside and above all these was the Church's conception of marriage as a mystery, a symbol, a sacrament. Yet even here a distinction had to be made. It could not be a sacrament in the ordinary sense, not a medium of grace, or else the giving of dower would be an act of simony, an attempt to buy the gifts of God with money. At a later date the Council of Trent was able to go further and lay down that it is a sacrament in the proper sense, a means of grace. But in the earlier centuries this loftier view was hampered by the need of protecting the principle of dower ; and this is an illustration of the way in which the spiritual view had to compromise with the material, the canonist make terms with the feudal lawyer.

The sacramental view of marriage which would make it indissoluble, and make it a matter solely for spiritual tribunals, was also confronted with a much lower practical and popular view, which forced undue attention to be given to the physical conditions ; in the cases, for example, of affinity

by illicit connexion, and of nullity on the ground
of impotence.   For this popular view seemed to be
often countenanced by scriptural texts : ' the two
are one flesh.'   On the other hand, important
consequences followed from marriage being a sacrament.   The first consequence was that marriage
must be accessible to all ; and thus the law of the
Church, after a long struggle with Roman law and
Teutonic   custom,   gradually   broke   down   the
harsher lines of parental control over children.
The   second   consequence   was   that   clandestine
marriages must not be annulled, but punished by
penance, for example.   The third consequence was
the equality of the sexes in regard to rights and
duties in marriage.   A fourth was the presumption
in favour of marriage, for instance if the parties
to a contract afterwards cohabited.

Difficul-   We might expect the sacramental view to have
ties.
another consequence, that marriage could only be
validly contracted *in facie ecclesiae*, as indeed was
laid down by the Eastern Church.   But we shall
see that there were good reasons why the Western
Church only worked slowly towards this position.

Again, if the Church took too hard a line in
laying down what should be the essentials of a
valid marriage, she would only defeat her own end
and increase the great danger of the time, irregular
and inferior forms of marriage.   Doubtless she was
also influenced by the characteristic mediaeval
belief in the efficiency of a formula *per se* ;   the

mystic words *in praesenti* (*magna est vis eorum*) could not well be supposed to have no efficiency, even if the utterer had no full qualification to pronounce them. In old English law, a tortious feoffment may have an effectual operation. So in the *Gemma*,[1] the sign of the Cross made by an unbelieving Jew avails to keep off the demons, much to their disgust. Hence the reluctance of *In facie ecclesiae.* the Church to lay down boldly the rule that a marriage not solemnized under Church conditions is null and void. But towards such a rule she was steadily working all the time. In Mangnall's *Questions*, we used to be instructed to reply to the question, When were marriages first solemnized in churches ? by saying, In the reign of King John. This is a distorted form of the fact that it was Innocent III who, at the Lateran Council of 1215, first laid down as a general rule what had already been adopted in parts of Christendom—as for example in England, where Archbishop Hubert, in 1200, at the Lambeth Council, 'saving the honour and privilege of the Church of Rome,' ordered the publication of banns three times before marriage. It was held indeed by the House of Lords in 1843[2] and in 1859[3], that the English Church had in this matter taken an independent and a bolder line ; that she had from the earliest times required for

[1] Giraldus Cambrensis, *Gemma Ecclesiastica.*
[2] *The Queen* v. *Millis* in 10 Clark and Finelly, p. 534.
[3] *Beamish* v. *Beamish* in House of Lords' Cases, ix. 289.

a valid marriage the presence of a clerk in orders.
But all of us, and not merely those who may be
members of the Scottish Free Kirk, would be
prepared to admit that the House of Lords can
sometimes be surprising. The House of Lords,
being the highest Appeal Court, can by its decisions
make law. But it must not claim to make history
too. The fuller documents now available for the
study of history make it impossible to accept this
decision of the House of Lords as a true statement
of historical fact. And the very hypothesis of such
independent action on the part of the English
Church in the eleventh, twelfth, and thirteenth
centuries is an instance of that misapprehension
of the true relation of England to Rome which
a student of mediaeval documents must needs
repudiate. On this point the famous decretal [1] of
Alexander III is conclusive. He decides that
a marriage duly solemnized and consummated is
invalidated by the fact that there had before been
verba de praesenti, ' I take you as mine,' between
the woman and another man, though this prior
contract had been accompanied by no religious
ceremony, and had not been consummated.

The Common Law. It is true that, when the common law judges lay
down as the condition of dower, that it shall have
been conferred *ad ostium ecclesiae*, they seem to be
insisting on the religious ceremony, even though
at the time (in Bracton's life) the Church had not

[1] *Compilatio Prima*, 4. 4 c. 6.

yet mustered courage to do so. But Professors Pollock and Maitland have clearly shown [1] that what the lawyers were insisting on was publicity, just as they did in their rules as to seisin and in their rejection of wills of land. In the same way the English common law diverged from the law of the Church when the barons in 1236, being asked to accept the Church doctrine *legitimatio per subsequens matrimonium*, that a subsequent marriage legitimated the children born before it, returned their famous answer, ' *Nolumus leges Angliae mutari.*' In the following century the lawyers carried their divergence further by rejecting the ' putative ' marriages allowed by the Church ; marriages, for example, where there was consanguinity and affinity between the parties though they had been unaware of it at the time. The lawyers also a century after Bracton's time came to reject the Church view of divorce as depriving the guilty wife of her dower ; they would only deprive her of her dower if the marriage was pronounced to have been a nullity from the beginning. All these divergences from Church law illustrate two points : the estrangement from the Church and hostility to its legislation which had become marked in England by the fourteenth century ; and the fact that, with all its hesitations and confusions, the Church view of marriage was

[1] *Hist. Eng. Law*, ii. 372–3.

more tolerant at once and more spiritual than the view taken by the lay world.

The distinction of *praesenti* and *futuro*.   One of the Church doctrines on the subject of marriage which ultimately did most harm was the importance, a factitious importance as it seems to us, attached to the distinction between *verba de praesenti* compared with *verba de futuro* ; ' I do now take you for my wife' compared with ' I promise to take you for my wife'. If after the former words the parties lived together, it was an indissoluble marriage. Even if they never lived together, the potency of the present tense had created an indissoluble bond which could break up any subsequent marriage of either of the two with a third person.[1] Luther spoke bitterly of the fooleries about *verba de praesenti* and *verba de futuro* which broke up many a marriage, and made out others to be marriages which were not really so.

Now it is true that the distinction is one which seems at first a singularly unreal piece of quibbling. It is true also that the distinction only grew up after the middle of the twelfth century; that it was the creation of the dialecticians of Paris University, and was stubbornly resisted by the lawyers of Bologna ; that it introduced an element of confusion and perplexity into the historic

[1] Peter Lombard, *Sentent.* iv, D, 27 c ' Si autem verbis explicant quod tamen corde non volunt, si non sit coactio ibi vel dolus, obligatio illa verborum . . . matrimonium facit.'

development of the law of marriage ; and that it placed a vast adjudicating and dispensing power in the hands of the Popes. Its practical working too, as shown in Alexander III's decision,[1] is decidedly startling. A woman had married a man with all publicity and solemnity, and she had lived as his wife with him. This marriage was declared null, because formerly, at the command of a lord, she had gone through a form of *desponsatio* with another man, not in the presence of a priest, nor with any of the ceremonies of marriage, and never living with him as a wife ; and the annulling turned on the fact that the words had been words *de praesenti* ; 'after such words she cannot and ought not to marry another.'

Yet this distinction grew by a natural development out of the various conceptions, Jewish, Roman, Teutonic, which the Church was fusing into one settled ascertainable code. The Jewish law attached great importance to betrothal. The essence of marriage in Roman law lay in the consensus followed by the *domum deductio*. Teutonic law, to give a man full power (*mund*) over his wife, required a betrothal of her by the parents in return for a price paid by the man. From all these sources came the *desponsatio* of the canonists. If was Peter Lombard who did most to enforce the great distinction between *sponsalia de praesenti*

---

[1] *Compilatio Prima*, 4. 94 c. 6 ; Friedberg, *Recht d. Ehe-schliessung*, p. 47.

and *sponsalia de futuro*.[1] His argument was that
a real consensus implies the here and now, and it
must be expressed by some recognized form of
words. If done in secret it would be still binding
in foro conscientiae ; to make it also legally binding
in foro externo, only required evidence. This
evidence would be supplied either by an open
avowal from the parties, or by their living together
as man and wife ; for this raised a presumption
which served as evidence of the former consensus.
By the thirteenth-century Popes it was laid down
that this presumption could not be rebutted or
traversed. *Sponsalia de futuro* can, on the other
hand, be thrown aside, though not by the parties
themselves. For after the twelfth century the
Church stepped in to check this licence of repudiation, and declared that persons must go to the
Pope for a dispensation, which in practice meant
applying to a Papal delegate empowered to hear
such cases.

Action
of the
Church.

This was surely a fair and reasonable marriage
law. The Church was bound to keep betrothal, but
she saw that if betrothal was to be so important
it must be strictly defined. Judaic and Teutonic
law had combined to introduce the custom of child
betrothals, and the property interests of feudalism

---

[1] The distinction between *verba de praesenti* and *verba de
futuro* was not the invention of Peter Lombard ; it is already
found in Hugh St. Victor, and in a decretal of Innocent II,
comp. *I de Spons.* iv. i.

clung to these. But the Church limited them by insisting on a minimum age of seven years, and by relegating them to the category of futurity, and qualifying them as promissory and dissoluble.

By this distinction between present and future, the marriage between Joseph and Mary ceased to be a stumbling-block ; it took its place as a true marriage, and symbolical, as all marriage was defined to be, of the spiritual union between Christ and the Church. Thus the Judaic view of marriage, with its Oriental grossness, was at last replaced by something both loftier and truer.

There was a great struggle between the old and the new theories, between the legists and the logicians, between Bologna and Paris. Was the *desponsatio* in either form to be regarded as a marriage, or only in the form of *verba de praesenti* ? The Paris Summa about 1165 says, it is not yet determined whether the Gallican Church usage or the Roman, that is, the older, the Bolognese, is the sounder. The Cologne Summa about the same date,[1] says :

'In this question the Gallican and Transalpine Churches are at variance ; the former rejects the eight causes which, according to Bologna, could dissolve a marriage, and insists against Bologna, that while the use of *verba de praesenti* constitutes a *desponsatio legalis*, *verba de futuro* only make a *desponsatio canonica* ; after the former there can be no other marriage ; after the latter there ought to be no other, just as contracts go by the meaning of words,

[1] Scheurl, *Eheschliessung*, § 22.

not by the secrets of conscience. . . . It is a conflict not
only of persons but of Churches. In the French Church
we were brought up in the faith, in the other instructed
in law. We must not wound either our mother or our
instructress. The Church of Rome, waiving its superior
authority and its power to issue decisions, deigns to enter
the lists with her daughter and meet her with weapons
of argument.'

The last words might seem to take a peculiar
line as to the supremacy of the Holy See. But the
context shows that the reference is not to the
Papacy, but to the Italian Church as against the
French, Bologna against Paris, and Canon Law
against scholastic theology.

When, therefore, as was the case up to about
1170, the very central definition of a marriage was
disputable, and the whole law of the subject was
in a state of rapid flux, the legislative activity of
the central authority becomes of prime importance.
Still more would this be the case, when among
the Popes of the next fifty years, three were great
Canon Law lecturers, Alexander III, Innocent III,
and Gregory IX. Thus Sicard of Cremona, writing
in 1180 on the question between Paris and Bologna,
The rule remarks[1] that the decrees of the Pope, Alexander III,
set by
Alexan- have now settled the question. It was settled in
der III. favour of the new theory. The new theory had
been maintained by the Pope while he was still
Magister Rolandus. Now that he is Pope he can
enforce his view on the whole world, ' whatever

[1] Freisen, op. cit., p. 190.

opposite views may be held by some persons, and may even have been laid down in judgements by some of my predecessors.'[1] But his object is not merely to use his new power, like Brennus's sword, to turn the scale in his own favour. He wants to fix a line after which the parties themselves cannot recede. This had been the reason why the Church at once took up Peter Lombard's distinction. Even before his distinction was promulgated, the Church of herself was tending that way, because the analogy of the law of property suggested that marriage should be completed by *traditio*, the handing over of the article ; and for *traditio*, words *de praesenti* appeared necessary. It seems as if Alexander III's decision[2] in the English case came early in his pontificate. It was a case by which the bare words *de praesenti*, without religious ceremony or cohabitation, were made adequate to constitute an indissoluble marriage. This would carry the new theory out to its extremest point. But later decisions modified this, and the general result is expressed in the decretals drawn up under Gregory IX. The only absolutely indissoluble marriage was a *matrimonium consummatum*. A *matrimonium non consummatum* might be voidable, but only through the action of the Pope ; the parties could not break it off except in the single case of either of them wanting to enter ' religion '.

[1] c. 3 X. iv. 4.
[2] c. 6 (8), comp. I. (iv. 4) ; c. 15, comp. I. (iv. 1).

What Alexander III then had done was to introduce the direct action of the Papacy as the sole
judge of doubtful marriages ; that is, he took
a great step towards securing the greatest of all
qualities about the law on any subject, that it be
ascertainable, uniform, and final. Thus the glossator
Huguccio, writing before the close of the twelfth
century, speaks of the bad old custom of letting
a man keep a second wife, when he ought really
to have been sent back to the first ; it had been
supported by Gratian without any warrant, ' but
now, thank God, by the authority of Alexander III
and Urban III, it has been abolished except that
it prevails in practice in the Bologna district.' [1]
But he did not carry the new theory to its extreme,
as the glossators would fain do. Here we see the
Papacy in the guise of a moderating influence
upon the more headlong, that is, the more logical
canonists. They go so far in making words *de
praesenti* enough to constitute a valid marriage,
that they declare consummation to be unnecessary
except for the incidental *tertium bonum* of off-
spring ; they reduce the eight causes which can
dissolve a marriage to three (nullity, affinity,
' religion ') ; they tend to the view that even the
former two of these can only affect a marriage
which has been made *per verba de futuro*.

The
Papacy
checks   Robert of Flamborough about 1207 [2] says the
decretals of Alexander III allow one of the parties

---

[1] c. 5 X. iv. 4.   [2] Ed. Schulte, 1868.

to a *sponsatio de praesenti* if unconsummated [1] the ex-
to enter religion, and the other party to marry tremists.
some one else ; *quod ego non audeo consulere.* He
has reached the logical climax ; *verba de praesenti*
make marriage, and marriage is indissoluble. But
there is such a thing in this world of makeshifts
as being too logical ; and there is certainly no use
in being more Papal than the Pope. The ecclesiastical left wing evidently required a good deal of
holding back.[2] Judaic law had imposed from the
first its very carnal view of marriage. It had also
imposed the view that betrothal is at least an
inchoate marriage. It became necessary to define
betrothal very exactly, and out of this necessity
had grown up the distinction between *de praesenti*
and *de futuro.* This scholastic distinction threatened at one time the whole historic development
from St. Augustine to Gratian. The scholastic
party was strong enough to force the Popes to
accept the distinction, but the Popes were strong
enough to prevent the distinction being pushed
to all its logical consequences. The price paid for
this compromise was a considerable amount of
confusion in the marriage law of the thirteenth
century, and a more than considerable amount of
invective against it in the Reformation century
and the two succeeding. But the part taken in
the compromise by the Popes between Gratian and

---

[1] This is a survival from the Bologna school, Esmein, i. 31.
[2] c. 2 X. i. 7 ; c. 7 X. iii. 32.

the Extra Decretum was a very reasonable part.
Alexander III laid down that if a mere betrothal
(*de futuro*) were followed by an actual cohabitation,
the law must presume that the parties meant it
as a marriage, and it could not be upset by a
subsequent marriage, even in terms *de praesenti*
and with cohabitation. Gregory IX laid down [1]
that this presumption of law was one that could
not be rebutted.

Papal appeals. Besides protecting the marriage law from the
extreme scholastics, the other benefit the Papacy
conferred in this half-century was the substitution
of an appeal to its central tribunal instead of
the unlicensed action of the interested parties.
A marriage might be voidable, it might have been
a mere promissory betrothal, or again it might
have been a betrothal never carried out though in
the present tense. But the parties could not of
themselves treat it as void till it had been declared
void by the head of the Church. It required his
dispensing power to declare them free of their
former obligations, and to assign the due penance
for breaking these.

There were other uses for dispensing power, which
have sometimes come in for still harder words.
It was freely used in dispensing from impediments
of consanguinity or blood-relationship,[2] and impediments of affinity or relationship through marriage.

[1] c. 30 X. iv. i.
[2] Coke (2nd Inst. 684) quotes the case of a man whose

But here again, in dealing with affinity, the Church had started with two ideas, a Roman and a Jewish, which it had to harmonize and to work into its system. The term 'affinity' came from Roman law, but the maxim 'They two shall be one flesh' was Judaic. Under the pressure of this maxim the Church assimilated affinity to consanguinity. St. Augustine had said, ' Si una caro sunt, nurus est filia.' Not only did the Church forbid the marriage to a deceased wife's sister, and the marriage to a deceased brother's wife, which Judaic law had countenanced or even ordered ; but the Church tried to make prohibition extend as far among *affines* as among *consanguinei,* that is to the seventh degree, and to enforce the same distinction between degrees that would annul a marriage and degrees that were only impediments. But she had in practice to make a large concession ; the penance within the degrees of consanguinity was heavier than within similar degrees of affinity.[1]

Misled by the figurative language of another text,[2] the Church developed the doctrine of *affinitas illegitima . . . de sola carnis commixtione nascitur* (Gratian, Bernhardus, Thomas Aquinas).

Here again the Papacy had to take the function marriage was annulled because of a prior intrigue with his future wife's third cousin.

[1] Robertus, Schulte, p. 18 ' Plus illum puniam qui accessit ad sororem suam quam illum qui ad duas sorores accessit.'

[2] 1 Cor. vi. 16 ' Qui adhaeret meretrici unum corpus efficitur.'

of compromise between the strict canonist rules and the laxity of worldly practice. Alexander III laid down [1] that affinity created thus by illicit action did annul marriage ; when he was only Master Roland he had remarked that the *rigor iusticiae* was not carried out in practice, especially as to *affinitas illegitima superveniens*. Successors of his in the Bologna chairs [2] were not afraid to criticize him outspokenly for his views of *affinitas illegitima superveniens*. Their language speaks eloquently of this body of professional opinion as a powerful force with which the Popes had to reckon. Now we can see why the Pope sent his decretals out to these experts for their approval. It was they who had forced him into harsher positions than he had taken as Magister, when he would not allow that this offence after marriage necessarily annulled the marriage ; now, as Pope, he declares it does annul marriage. Even when he yields, as in case of a man guilty with his wife's sister, he says it could only be purged by pilgrimage to Jerusalem ; and the story is to be hushed up (*dissimulatum*).

When the Popes do relax the rules, they have to do it at first under cover of the professional distinctions between the different degrees of affinity,

[1] c. 2 X. iv. 13.
[2] Robert of Flamborough : ' Nonne hoc iniquitas ? . . . Ego dico quod si velit uxor retinere maritum, non est ab eo separanda usque ad tertium gradum sive manifestum, sive occultum.'

between a notorious and a non-notorious case, between witting and unwitting offenders. Not till Innocent IV did they feel strong enough to come out from these shelters and boldly pronounce that a valid marriage was not annulled by *affinitas illegitima*, but only that the guiltless partner may live apart from the guilty one.

In the same spirit at the Lateran Council 1215, Innocent III had cut away that extension of affinity in the second and third genus, in which the canonists had revelled. They had made affinity in the first genus prohibitory to the seventh degree, to three degrees in the second genus, and to two degrees in the third genus. Henceforth only the first genus was considered; and only up to the fourth degree was it to be regarded as invalidating a marriage unless a direct dispensation were given.

The Papacy had to play a similar rôle in moderating the doctrine of 'spiritual kinship'. Here too a doctrine had been elaborated out of a few texts. To enter the Kingdom,[1] a man must be born again of water and the Spirit ; and St. Paul calls Titus and Timothy his sons. If baptism is a birth, then those who stand together at the font are close kindred. I cannot marry my goddaughter ; my son cannot marry her. But if a man and a woman have been godparents together, can their children marry ? Tancred[2] answers this question and

Spiritual affinity.

---

[1] John iii. 5.   [2] Tancred (ed. Wunderlich), p. 36.

others by remitting it to Rome, ' The point is
new, and therefore the Pope should be consulted
on it.'   Alexander III [1] had allowed diversities of
local custom. The canonists objected : ' Is a mere
local custom to disjoin those whom God hath
joined ? ' One famous authority (Huguccio) [2] says,
' This is not a decretal, or if it is, then he spoke not
as Pope, but as professor.'   The Glossator calls
attention to this, ' Note that here he finds fault
with the Pope.'   But, after all, the canonists were
setting up the Holy See against local custom, they
were defending the Pope against himself ; and to
find fault in such a cause was a subtle flattery.

There was even one party at Rome [3] which
wished to apply the analogy of baptism to confirmation and to confession. The last had considerable practical importance, because in urgent
need a layman could hear confession. The Sire de
Joinville might forget all the sins confessed by his
friend the Constable of Cyprus, but the Church
would not forget that there had been a confession,
and it might be awkward if they found they had
become blood-relations, so that no member of the
one family could marry into the other, and that
if they did there was *impedimentum dirimens*.
A further subtlety lay in the doctrine of *cognatio
spiritualis superveniens*. If a father acted as
sponsor to his own son, he became spiritually a near

[1] c. 3 X. iv. 11.   [2] Gloss. on c. 3 X. iv. 11.
[3] Freisen, op. cit., p. 538, note 5.

relation of his own wife ; must he not therefore
separate from her ?   Alexander III had the good
sense to say no ; it was only an *impedimentum
impediens* and could not annul a marriage already
subsisting.   There were doctors, again, who tried
to work in the Roman law principles of adoption.
But the Popes never gave in to this.   Again, the
schools were powerful enough to enforce on their
Papal legislators the rule they worked out by the
early thirteenth century, that while marriage to
a non-Christian was null, marriage to a heretic
was valid once contracted.   On the other hand,
Papal legislation rejected the attempt to regard
any one of five or six crimes as heinous enough to
dissolve a marriage.   Innocent III followed Alexander III as against the ruling of Clement III,[1]
and excluded all but two cases, the case where
there had been adultery with plotting death, or
the case of adultery with promise of subsequent
marriage.   Nor could the Popes be induced to
follow the Romanist views in making it *infamia*
for a widow to marry within the year, or in
attaching penalties to a second marriage.   And
Clement III in particular abolished the old theory
that the prohibited seasons within which marriages
could not be celebrated should include from
Septuagesima to the octave of Whit Sunday ;
(which this year, for instance, would be from
February 11 to June 10).   Even so this prohibition

[1] c. 4, 5 X. iv. 7.

was to be *impedimentum impediens* not *dirimens*.[1] In each of these questions the Papacy is a correcting and restraining force.

Otherwise, these doctrines of consanguinity and affinity had certainly been stretched to a point that proved impracticable. Already by 1215 Innocent III recognized this; he reduced the prohibitory force of consanguinity from the seventh degree to the fourth, and refused to make affinity prohibitory beyond the first genus.[2] The canonical rules were no doubt more often a dead letter in this than in any other sphere. Moreover, this graduated scale of sinfulness introduced a most undesirable casuistry into a social region which beyond all others is beset with temptation, and which needs to be kept straightforward and pure beyond all others. Nor was there any region in which the power of dispensation was so dangerous and so demoralizing. Yet it is only fair to say, that the too lofty ideal set up by the Church expressed the horrified recoil of the highest minds from what seemed to them shocking and incestuous laxity. We must never forget that the Middle Ages had only just emerged from barbarian society. The sensuality, the violence, the gross materialism that were still all about them provoked protests

The motives of the Church.

---

[1] The Gloss. on c. un. X. iv. 12 'dicunt quidam quod non dissolvitur matrimonium cum illud impedimentum sit temporale. Uguccio dicit quod non est matrimonium nec obstat quod temporale est impedimentum.'

[2] c. 9 X. iv. 14.

that seem to us exaggerated. From such protests came the exaltation of a fantastic chastity, a fantastic quietism, an unnatural spirituality. We have to enter into these ages, to breathe their very air, to feel their sense that beneath the thin crust of social order and religion there lay the slumbering fires of a bloodthirsty and licentious paganism, before we can understand the canon law of marriage, the sacrosanctity of the clergy, the spread of monasticism.

Another trial of strength between the Papacy and the profession took place over the vow of celibacy. This was regarded by the early Church as a spiritual marriage to the heavenly spouse. It therefore precluded any later marriage. This doctrine was connected with the development of clerical celibacy and the spread of monasticism. It was therefore rapidly worked up by the canonists in and after the twelfth century, especially when they got hold of one of the distinctions in which they delighted. This was the distinction between a simple vow and a solemn vow, by means of which they made St. Augustine say that though the former was not an *impedimentum dirimens,* yet the solemn vow was. They also identified the solemn vow with the *desponsatio per verba de praesenti,* and the simple vow with the *verba de futuro* ; and the first decade of the thirteenth century versified the rule in the ' Marrow of Matrimony '.[1] ' Nam

The vow of celibacy.

---

[1] Schulte, *Beitrag.* iii.

solemne solet de praesenti profiteri. Ast de venturo
simplex vult usque voveri, . . . Copula legitima
per simplex non dirimetur.'

Alexander III had seemed to discredit this
identification ; therein, says Huguccio,[1] he must
be taken to speak not as Pope, but only his own
opinion as Professor, and the Pope cannot give
dispensation from such a solemn vow. This last
maxim was laid down by Innocent III himself ;
poverty and chastity are so essential a part of the
monastic life, that not even the Pope can dispense
from them. But the general feeling was that
Papal power is too great to have limits set upon
it even by the Pope ; and the gloss on this passage
is that it can only mean, that if the Pope does
dispense a man from these vows it must be done
by setting him free from the monastery altogether ;
' others hold that the *plenitudo potestatis* does
give the Pope power to issue this dispensation.' [2]
This last position had to be accepted by later Popes;
but they were able to hold out against the extreme
canonists' strict interpretation of all such vows,
and to decide that an *impedimentum dirimens* only
came from the solemn vow, not the simpler,[3] and
only when the solemn vow had been followed up
by taking orders above that of subdeacon, or by
entering religion.[4]

The implied vow of celibacy played a great part

---

[1] Schulte, *Litt.-Geschichte*, p. 43.   [2] c. 6 X. iii. 35.
[3] c. 6 X. iv. 6 ; c. 6 X. iv. 15.   [4] c. un. de Voto VI°. iii. 15.

in determining the rule of celibacy for the clergy. Celibacy of the clergy. This is a question which hardly receives unprejudiced treatment from English historians. If any one were to argue at the present day that single-minded devotion to a profession or an art is hindered by matrimony, he would probably be told first, that the statement is untrue ; second, that family life is of more vital importance to a society and to any normal member of it, than is any profession or art ; thirdly, that celibacy, generally speaking, is a condition at once selfish, unpatriotic, and morally dangerous. And each of these objections would, no doubt, be valid in our present society. Yet it is more than probable that any real familiarity with the early Middle Ages will lead an unprejudiced student to the belief that the celibacy of the clergy was at that time essential to the setting apart of a clerical order, to the purification of the Church, and to its influence upon the world ; that clerical celibacy was in fact a necessary stage in the spiritualization of European society. Now powerful as was the work done Its growth. by the Hildebrandine Popes to help on clerical celibacy, yet still more was done to fix and develop the doctrine by the canon lawyers. It was they who extended the rule to include subdeacons. Alexander III had pronounced that subdeacons were not to be regarded as being in orders of the higher grade.[1] He had even given a dispensation

[1] c. 2 X. iv. 6.

to a subdeacon to be married. This particular
case proved a great stone of offence. The famous
commentator Huguccio says, ' The man must have
never been baptized, or been too illiterate for
orders, or must have uncanonically skipped some
grades.' [1] Another commentator suggests that we
can get over the case by holding that the clerk is
bound to celibacy, not by his vow on ordination,
but by the rule of Church discipline, from which the
Pope *can* give a dispensation, whereas from the
vow he cannot. Another has heard that this
particular dispensation had not been issued with
the Pope's full privity, and he gets over it thus.
But get over it somehow they are all agreed we
must. For they are bound at all costs to save the
principle of the vow, for this has become the
recognized way of meeting the awkward text [2] in
the Epistle to Timothy, ' Let a bishop be the husband of one wife.' Here and in 1 Corinthians [3] the
apostle Paul had given priests the right to marry,
but he also said that celibacy was the better way ;
and by the very fact of taking orders it was said
the priest chooses to abandon this right ; for a
vow of celibacy is now annexed to ordination and
implied in it, and every priest is aware of this
when he takes orders. The conflict here between

Conflict
with the
plenitudo
potestatis.
two rapid new growths, clerical celibacy and the
Papal *plenitudo potestatis*, is very interesting.

[1] Freisen, op. cit., p. 758.   [2] 1 Tim. iii. 2.
[3] 1 Cor. vii. 8.

' I have heard it argued', says Robert of Flamborough,[1] ' that the Pope could give dispensation to marry even to a priest or a Cistercian abbot. But saving the reverence due to my Lord the Pope, what I have laid down is the sounder view.' That there was such a divergence of views is partly due to the remarkable fact that till Boniface VIII the Church never positively enacted that orders annul marriage. This was accepted as a principle by Gregory IX, but direct legislation to this effect was avoided, because it was felt that marriage was *iure naturae*, was a right of which no one could divest a man, it required his own act thereto. In the fourteenth century it was still disputed which was the element in orders which annuls a marriage ; was it the vow, or, as the greatest of all commentators, John Andreae, held, was it the Church rule ?—a question which even the Council of Trent left undetermined.

In the matter of divorce, the Church started with Divorce. an aim to work for, that marriage is indissoluble. ' Whom God hath joined together, let not man put asunder.' [2] Only two exceptions had the New Testament allowed : adultery, and the desertion by an unbelieving partner.[3] But both the Judaic and the Roman law had allowed divorce to a degree that has been called ' unbridled licence ',[4] and Teutonic custom had recognized many causes

---

[1] Ed. Schulte, p. 7.   [2] Matt. xix. 6.
[3] I Cor. vii. 15.   [4] Esmein, ii. 46.

for separation, such as blindness, leprosy, insanity, captivity. It cost the Church a long struggle of eleven centuries to overcome all these systems, for its sole coercive weapon was penance. But by the time of Gratian the principle was achieved. There may for good cause be separation *a mensa et toro* ; but the actual *vinculum matrimonii* can never be broken asunder. What seems a divorce in this full sense, is strictly only a declaration that the marriage was null, from the beginning, that there had been no *vinculum*. But here again the clear view taken in Gratian's Decretum was broken into confusion by Peter Lombard's scholastic distinction of *praesenti* and *futuro*. Thus Bernard asks the question, ' Can a wife enter religion against her husband's will ? ' If the formula is spoken in the present tense, this makes a marriage, and marriage is indissoluble ; so the answer ought to have been no, she cannot. And to this answer he inclines. But the Church inclined to say yes ; and he has to conclude with the words, *Adhuc sub iudice lis est.* Scholasticism we have seen was a mighty influence, but monasticism we see was even

Papal compromises.

mightier. The Popes took up a reasonable line. A couple can agree to separate, but both must agree, and both must enter religion. ' This has been so settled by the present Pope after long controversy,' says Sicard of Cremona, 1180, referring to Alexander III.[1] The same Pope pronounced

[1] c. 4 X. iii. 32.

that not even for leprosy could one partner desert
the other unless by consent;[1] a heroic view of
conjugal duty, but heroic views were just what the
twelfth century needed in every sphere. In the
same spirit the Church had disallowed the old right
of an injured husband to act for himself, he must
sue in due form and await judgement of the courts.
The Church had set up seven or eight pleas by
which a guilty wife might save herself from judicial
separation, such pleas as the husband's cognizance,
or his having been reputed dead, or his condoning
the offence, or his being equally guilty. For the
Church maxim was equality of treatment for the
two sexes : *non ad imparia iudicantur, eadem lex
viro et mulieri.* This is perhaps Utopian, but it is
at any rate above the gross onesidedness of both
Judaic and Roman law, which, for instance, had
made even Gratian say, ' The wife cannot bring
an accusation against her husband, for so runs the
Roman law.' But the Popes had allowed fairer
treatment. They had also allowed the guiltless
to receive back the guilty party after penance,
a concession to the indissolubleness of marriage,
but also a concession to social peace and common
sense.

This view of marriage as indissoluble was perhaps
too high an ideal for the society of the time. But
that is just another of the cases in which the high
pitch of the ideal measures the recoil from low

[1] c I and c. 2 X. iv. 8.

practice. It was so high-pitched that the Church herself could not fully act up to it, and had to temporize and compromise. But it is evident that there is some unfairness in summing up the Church view of marriage as low, and simultaneously complaining of it as impracticably high. It was high just as the monastic ideal was high, and for the same reason and with similar results. It was above the men of that age ; they could not attain unto it ; but it held up a lofty conception before their eyes.

The children.
In the treatment of the children of a marriage, the modern world has come round almost wholly to the attitude taken up by the mediaeval Church. Instead of making illegitimacy the inevitable consequence of any failure in legal conditions on the part of the parents, she confined it to cases where the parents had been guilty. In fact she took an equitable view of the legal situation. She legitimated all children of 'putative' marriages, i.e. those solemnized by the Church and with *bona fides* of the parties.[1] This was emphatically decreed both by Alexander III and by Innocent III. In so decreeing they had to run counter to some of the leading canonists, like Robert of Flamborough, who had only allowed such children to be legitimate for purposes of inheritance and for pleading in secular courts, but not for Holy Orders or for ecclesiastical courts. Huguccio had even insisted on a refinement which has been happily called a lopsided

[1] c. 2 and c. 14 X. iv. 17.

legitimacy ; where one parent had married in *bona fides*, the other not, the child would be legitimate on the one side and not on the other. The same canonist had resisted the doctrine of legitimation by subsequent marriage of the parents ; he would let such children inherit but not take orders. Here again Alexander III boldly gave the doctrine its wider scope.[1] *Matrimonium omnia precedentia purgat.* He could force it upon the Church, but it could not be forced upon the stubborn English baronage at Merton in 1236 ; *nolumus leges Angliae mutari.*

Boniface VIII enounced that the Pope has all laws in his breast. But this full development of the theory had only been reached by a long process. Gratian had said in the Decretum that the Pope can override any canon laws because he represents Christ, who was *dominus legis.* Yet some glossators stigmatized the chapter declaring the consequent Papal powers of dispensation as *capitulum difficile et famosum.* But Gratian's principle was bound to gain ground. It was the only way to effect his great purpose, the *concordantia discordantium canonum.* It was also a consequence of the scale he set up, in which the Bible, the first four Councils (some said the first eight Councils), the Pope, the Fathers, the rules of the Church, formed a descending series of authorities. It was also a corollary from the

The dispensing power.

[1] c. 13 X. iv. 17.

doctrine that the Pope was God's vicegerent upon earth. Such a power must be able to make new laws. And the social and moral progress of Christendom, as men felt and said, depended upon such new laws being made. Hence it has to be expressly postulated that a Pope can revoke the decrees of his predecessors ; ' they cease that moment to be decrees,' is the explanation of one glossator.[1] Of course an authority absolute and illimitable in theory may, and must in practice, have very tangible limitations. But these also must be made to square with the theory. The different churches of Christendom had very wide divergences in practice, but the hypothesis had to be made that these divergences only exist by a tacit licence from the Pope. The canonist will often have to reject a Papal ruling ; but the rejection will be salved with the formula that herein he spoke not as Pope but as professor, and a mediaeval was even more accustomed than a modern university to hear one professor refuting another, especially when the subject-matter was law. When Innocent III sent his new decretals to Bologna, he appealed to them not as supreme pastor to his flock, but as a professional to his fellows in the profession ; ' I send them to you that you may be able to apply them when need arises, in court and in the lecture-room.'[2] Honorius III was bolder, and issued his as law. Gregory IX went

---

[1] c. 25 q. 1 v. Contra Statutum.   [2] Potthast, 4157.

further and revoked all others. This left only one step to the full theory, the step which Boniface VIII took, *iura omnia in scrinio pectoris*.

In no subject was it so important to have a unity English opinions. of practice throughout Christendom as in the subject of marriage. Nor, again, was there any Church in Christendom so liable to become insular and unprogressive as the Church in the British Isles. It was of great value, therefore, that it is an English canonist who, even before Gregory IX's compilation of the Extra-Decretum, admitted in the plainest terms the Papal power to legislate and to issue dispensations in matrimonial cases. Richard le Poer, Bishop of Durham (1228-37) refers [1] to the limitations assigned to Papal power by his countryman, Robert of Flamborough, thirty years earlier ; the Gospel, the law of nature, the first four Councils, the canon law, had been the limiting principles assigned. But the later writer points out that precedents exist for the overriding of each one of these limits.

The frequency with which this passage is quoted by the later glossators shows how completely the older doctrines had given way, the doctrines that the Pope was bound by his predecessors, that canon rules admitted of no exceptions. The new idea of dispensing power had risen in response to a real need. It was the safety-valve of the now centralized machinery.

[1] Schulte, *Litt.-Geschichte*, p. 31.

Mediaeval marriage law came in for severe criticism at the Reformation. The Statute of 1540 (32 H. 8, c. 38) speaks of

Henry VIII's feelings.

' the usurped power of the Bishop of Rome . . . making that unlawful which by God's law is lawful. . . . Many persons long married and often with children . . . on pretence of precontract not consummated, on mere evidence of two witnesses were divorced . . . by other prohibitions than God's law admitteth, for their lucre by that court invented, the dispensation whereof they always reserved to themselves . . . all because they would get money by it and keep a reputation to their usurped jurisdiction . . . whereby many just marriages have been undone and lawful heirs disinherited. . . .

Marriages have been brought into such uncertainty that no marriage could be so surely knit and bounden but it should lie in either of the parties' power and arbitre, casting away the fear of God, by means and compasses to prove a precontract, a kindred, an alliance, or a carnal knowledge. . . .

We declare all marriages lawful that be not prohibited by God's law or the Levitical degrees, that are contract and solemnized in the face of the Church and consummate with bodily knowledge or children . . . notwithstanding any precontract not consummate and notwithstanding any dispensation, &c.'

Henry VIII has no doubt some claim to express an opinion on the marriage laws. With him, as has been wittily said, marriage almost degenerated into a habit. But in this preamble he is also voicing the criticism of the Reformers, who denounced the canon law for facilitating clandestine marriages, for allowing marriages of infants, for the rules of kinship and affinity, for the conflicts between Church rules and State rules, and for the conflicts even inside the Church sphere, between the *forum internum* and the *forum externum*,[1] and finally for the insistence on celibacy of the clergy though a confessed imposture. Luther's words on the subject are well known. Calvin's, as not so familiar, may be quoted verbatim : Calvin.

' Dum e matrimonio sacramentum fecerunt, ubi id semel obtinuere, coniugalium causarum cognitionem ad se traxerunt, quippe res spiritualis erat profanis iudicibus non attrectanda. Tum leges sanxerunt quibus tyranni-dem suam firmarunt, sed partim in Deum manifeste impias, partim in homines iniquissimas. Quales sunt : ut coniugia inter adolescentes, quae parentum iniussu contracta sunt, dissolvantur. Gradus vero ipsos contra gentium omnium iura et Mosis quoque politiam confingunt. Ne viro, qui adulteram repudiaverit, alteram inducere liceat. Ne spirituales cognati matrimonio copulentur. Ne a Septuagesima ad octavas Paschae, tribus hebdomadibus ante natalem Iohannis, ab Adventu ad Epiphaniam nuptiae celebrentur ; et similes innumerae quas recensere longum fuerit.'

The Reformers did the great service of vindica-ting matrimony as an honourable state, indeed as the ' truly religious condition '. But they reintro-duced the variability according to local customs, which, even if endurable now that Europe has broken up into nations, was illogical and intolerable when Europe was Christendom. Calvin, rejecting These attacks ignore histori-cal deve-lopment.

---

[1] Hostiensis, *Summa de Matrimonio*, p. 355 ; Friedberg, *Recht d. Eheschliessung*, p. 102.

the interpretation of μυστήριον by *sacramentum*,
naturally rejects the consequences of the sacramental view.   Ignoring the historic development
of the canonical rules, he does not see that they
represent, as it were, so many lines of escape from
worse conditions.   But he does avoid the mistake,
often made by some modern writers, of attributing
to the Church itself these bad conditions, amid
which it moved, against which it had striven, but
with which it sometimes had to palter and to
compromise.

His Tudor majesty's indictment admits of some
criticism, more than would have been safe in his
lifetime.   The ' pretence of precontract ' refers to
the *de praesenti* and *de futuro* distinction ; but the
main element in this was its attempt to spiritualize
existing views of matrimony by transferring the
stress from copula to consensus ; and the distinction made it possible to undermine many existing
abuses.   As to the ' prohibitions invented by Rome
for lucre ', most of these were far more stringent
and more unreasonable before the later twelfth
century—that is, before Rome, through Alexander III and his successors, established a Papal
control over the canonist schools.   The ' dispensations reserved to themselves ' were far better in
the hands of one central authority than left to
each individual bishop, or to the dubious con-
scientiousness of the interested parties, as was the
former practice.   The ' frequent disinheriting of

lawful heirs ' was an argument that might be met by a *tu quoque,* for no decisions could be more monstrous than some of those deduced from the presumptions of the common law.[1] ' By means and compasses to prove a precontract, kindred, &c.' is a complaint of the number of *impedimenta dirimentia.* But these it had been the marked policy of Rome to cut down and reduce in number, from their maximum of sixteen to only three or even one. As to ' parties casting out the fear of God ', it was something to have put into them a fear of the Church, and it certainly was not within ' their own powers and arbitre ' as much as it had been before, but a good deal less so.

But we have also to face a weighty indict-ment recently brought against the canon law of marriage. Mait-land's censure.

' Behind these intricate rules there is no deep policy, there is no strong religious feeling ; they are the idle ingenuities of men who are amusing themselves by inventing a game of skill which is to be played with neatly drawn tables of affinity and doggerel hexameters. The men and women who are the pawns in this game may if they be rich enough evade some of the forfeits by obtaining Papal dispensations ; but there must be another set of rules marking off the dispensable from the indispensable impediments. When we weigh the merits of the mediaeval Church and have remembered all her good deeds, we have to put into the other scale, as a weighty counterpoise, the incalculable harm done by a marriage-

---

[1] e.g. the presumption of access *in absentia.*

law which was a maze of flighty fancies and misapplied logic.' [1]

No one who has had the patience to follow the canon law of marriage in its historic development will be able to admit this as anything like a fair description. There assuredly was strong religious feeling behind its rules as these grew up. If they were afterwards administered with idle ingenuity, and in the spirit of a game of skill, this is the common experience of what happens when abstract principles are minted into current coin or even into counters, and the fault must be divided between human nature in general, and the class of lawyers in particular. The tables of kinship and affinity are due to the inconvenient honesty of taking the Bible, and the Bible in its most literal sense, as authoritative. As if the load of Judaic tradition, of Roman law, and of Teutonic custom were not enough, the set of texts and the scriptural examples which had to be worked into a rational system with all these materials made a task of almost impossible complexity. That a rational system was evolved is due to the concentration on this object of the most powerful minds for continuous centuries. That the technical rules were forced into memorial verses, was because they were required for constant use ; they had to be portable and handy. There was a time, many of us can remember it, when even the Thirty-nine Articles (*horresco referens*) were compressed into

---

[1] Pollock and Maitland, *Hist. Eng. Law*, ii. 387.

doggerel hexameters ; but the historic significance of the Thirty-nine Articles was not vitiated thereby. That the forfeits might be evaded by those who were rich enough was not peculiar to this branch of law. Something of the kind was said of the English marriage law, long after Giant Pope had ceased to hold that demesne. Indeed, in the prejudices of the vulgar, something of the kind is said of law in general, even in our own favoured times and in our own favoured land.

The flighty fancies, the misapplied logic, were the very things against which we see the Papacy setting its face consistently, brushing them away for sound sense and practical compromise. The maze was none of its making, and, compared with what existed before, was like an Italian garden compared to a tropical jungle.

Can it seriously be maintained that this should outweigh all the good done by the mediaeval Church, that institution which was the saviour of society after the barbarian deluge ? Is this one consideration to be really a counterpoise to all the religion, all the art, and most of the literature of the Middle Ages, to outweigh the names of Bede and Anselm, Langton and Grosseteste ?

The Pope, we know, can be fallible when he speaks not *ex cathedra*. Bishop Stubbs has been convicted by Professor Maitland of making some confusion between the attitude of the English State towards an order from Rome, and the attitude of the English Church towards the same order. But has Professor Maitland quite sufficiently distinguished between mediaeval Church and mediaeval society in general, when he holds the former responsible for abuses that were forced upon it by the latter ?

And is there not a further distinction to be made, which we cannot but wish more emphasized in his brilliant lectures on the Canon law, a distinction which is essential to the true appreciation of the history of the Papacy, the distinction between the activity of the canonist schools and the activity of the Popes themselves, the distinction between the bar and the bench ?

Summary of Papal action upon marriage law.

It appears from this survey, first, how vastly important was the function of the Papacy as a final legislative authority upon all these intricate points, so vitally important for society to have incontestably settled. Second, how no authority less tremendous than the Vicar of God could have silenced the canonist schools and curbed their exuberant logic. Thirdly, how much the Papacy represents good practical sense and workable compromise. Fourthly, how steadily it pressed in the direction of reducing the number of *causae dirimentes* and relegating them into the list of *causae impedientes*. Fifthly, how little Henry VIII's preamble or Luther's Table Talk does justice to the real conditions of the marriage law, or at any rate its historic development up to the thirteenth century.

It cannot be said that the results were wholly Comparison with English law. satisfactory when the English law did take a line independent of the canon law, for it then rejected putative marriages and the *legitimatio per subsequens matrimonium,* and so refused to accept as good enough for heirship of lands children who were already good enough for heirship of movables and for holy orders. In fact we cannot feel clear that the common lawyer is qualified to throw the first stone at the canonist, when we think of the many blots on the history of the English marriage law, such as the wide variance between the English law and the Scottish with Gretna Green on the frontier between the two ; the iniquities of a system which produced Fleet marriages by making the essentials to consist in such externalities as the banns, the licence, the celebrant's possessing of orders ; and finally some unlovely aspects of Divorce Court procedure.

But without coming down to modern times, the common law of the Middle Ages had its paradoxes no less than the canon law. Thus it encouraged infant marriages by allowing a claim of dower from a child nine years old against a boy of four.[1] It countenanced the open sale of the *maritagium* or lord's right to dispose in marriage of heir or heiress in his wardship. It would not debar from dower [2]

---

[1] Coke on Littleton, 13a, compared with c. 2 X. iv. 2.

[2] Year Book, 32–3, Ed. I, p. 63 ; Magna Vita S. Hugonis, 170–7, quoted in Pollock and Maitland, ii. 390.

even a guilty wife separated *a mensa et toro*. By a preposterous stretching of a metaphor it gave an actual advantage to illegitimacy ; a bastard being *nullius filius* could not be the son of a serf and therefore must be always a free man.[1] It made the freedom or servitude of children of a freeman and a bondwoman depend on a triviality, whether the house was his or hers.[2] It set up so powerful a presumption in favour of legitimacy of children born as long as husband and wife are not divorced, that this presumption was allowed even to override the confession of the guilty party,[3] and heirs were foisted on an estate when they were confessedly illegitimate.

After indulging in such extravagances, is the English common law entitled to scoff at the ' maze ' of canon law and rebuke the ' flighty fancies ' of the canonists ? When one set of legal authorities thus takes to castigating another set, the mere historical student has to stand aside in respectful embarrassment. But he is tempted to ask, ' *Quis tulerit Gracchos de seditione querentes ?* '

---

[1] Year Book, 10 Ed. III, f. 35 (Tr. f. 24). Coke on Littleton, 32a, 32b, 235a.   [2] Bracton, f. 5, 194ʰ.

[3] The case in Pollock and Maitland, ii. 396 and 390.

LECTURE III

CHURCH AND STATE: GROSSETESTE AND
THE UNITY OF CHRISTENDOM

OF all the sayings about the Papacy, is there any more true, more suggestive, and withal more appreciative than the famous epigram by the greatest foe to hierarchical power that ever lived : 'If a man consider the original of this great ecclesiastical dominion, he will easily perceive that the Papacy is no other than the ghost of the deceased Roman Empire, sitting crowned upon the grave thereof.'

This saying of Hobbes hits the very central fact about the Empire of the Gregories and the Innocents, that it was a translation into spiritual terms of the Empire of the Caesars. It defeated the Hohenstauffen because compared with it they were but pretenders to that mighty inheritance ; they were barbarians, tribal chiefs, feudal figure-heads, when brought into juxtaposition with the classicism, the world-wide sway, the autocracy of Rome.

No wonder that the Middle Ages portrayed their relative importance by the contrast of sun to moon, soul to body, heaven to earth. It was inevitable that as the Church became more and more an organized state, the ordinary state should acquire a certain shade of the unspiritual and the profane. As the *civitas Dei* became a realized system, its rival necessarily sank into the *civitas seculi,* and with nothing before it but the alternative to figure either as a satellite to the kingdom of light or as a confessed kingdom of darkness. Already to Innocent III the *sacerdotium* is of God's ordinance, the *regnum* is of man's contriving. To the support of this view no one ever brought a more intense

Grosse-
teste on
the Pa-
pacy ;

conviction than did Grosseteste. In his eyes not only all Christians, but the whole human race, are bound to be subject to the Holy See, and no one can be saved who does not fulfil this ; it has the office of bringing salvation to the whole world. What a monstrous perversion, then, is that which sees in Grosseteste nothing but a harbinger of the Protestant Reformation, and which harps perpetually on a letter in which he is supposed to meet a direct Papal order with flat mutiny ; *non*

com-
pared
with
Matthew
Paris.

obedio, contradico, rebello. This letter we owe in the first instance to Matthew Paris, in whose summing-up of his character the same note is twice struck. The holy Bishop of Lincoln, who was the chastiser of prelates, the corrector of monks, the director of priests, the trainer of clerks, the supporter of scholars, the preacher of the people, the persecutor of the unchaste, the diligent student of the Scriptures, was also the open confuter of the Pope, the hammerer and despiser of the Romans.

It is Matthew Paris, again, who makes the dead

Bishop, coming in a vision by night, smite the Pope with his pastoral staff, so that he never had a day's health thereafter. He had said, if we believe the chronicler, ' Rejoice, all sons of the Church of Rome, for my two great enemies are dead, King Conrad and the Bishop of Lincoln ; ' and he had written to Henry III to get the Bishop's bones cast out of the church. Is this the true light in which to regard Grosseteste ?

There is a glaring contrast between Grosseteste's words of devout submission on the one hand, and on the other the picture drawn by Paris and the language of the letter. Let us examine this contrast a little closer ; it will bring us to the innermost convictions of Grosseteste on the subject of the Papacy's functions and services and on the question of setting bounds to Papal power ; that is, we shall be able to measure what hold the Papacy had on the best men of the time, and to discover how and why that hold began to relax.

The famous letter is said by Matthew Paris [1] to have been written to Innocent IV, and is so given in Grosseteste's letters.[2] But as the Vatican Register shows, it was sent to 'Magistro Innocentio domini Papae scriptori in Anglia commoranti ', as the Burton Annalist [3] rightly puts it. The form of address to a Pope is ' beatorum pedum oscula ',

The famous letter.

---

[1] *Hist. Maior*, v. 389, &c., vi. 229, &c.
[2] Grosseteste, *Epistolae*, ed. Luard, no. cxxviii.
[3] p. 432.

whereas the form ' noverit discretio vestra ' is that
which the Pope employs to his own notary.

It opens without any of his invariable courteous
approaches to a difficult subject, and plunges
bluntly into his objections. ' Be it known to
your discretion that to the Apostolic commands
I yield with the affection of a son in all respects
devout and reverent obedience ; but to those
points which are opposed to Apostolic commands
I offer, out of zeal for the honour of my father,
resistance and opposition ; to each of these courses
I am bound equally and alike by divine command.'

The phrases used are exaggerations of Grosseteste's own in other places ; e. g. the phrases that
' those who introduce into Christ's flock these
murderers are near akin to Lucifer and to Antichrist ; ' that ' this abuse of power by the Holy
See is a sitting down by the side of the powers of
darkness in the pestilential seat of the pains of
Hell.' There are awkward repetitions ; ' the power
given for edification not for destruction ' comes
thrice, ' the abominable sin pernicious to the
human race ' comes twice. The conclusion is
abrupt and violent ; ' in all filial obedience I refuse
obedience, I contradict, I rebel,' and at the close
the text is very awkwardly worked in, that ' these
provisions are things which flesh and blood have
revealed and not our Father which is in Heaven '.

It is unlike Grosseteste to lay down, with no
philosophical and scriptural arguments to back

it up, so new a proposition, so startlingly at variance with his own maxim often repeated that to resist a Papal order is as the sin of witchcraft. It is unlike his procedure in similar circumstances to make no reference at all to the facts of the case, the youth of the presentee, his foreignness, &c. Compare it with the letter which comes His other nearest to it in regard to these facts, letter xlix to letters. Cardinal Otto. In this he begins by the most emphatic assertion possible that his obedience to the Holy See is not the compulsion of fear but the proffer of love ; that, please God, nothing shall avail to part him from it, neither tribulation nor straits nor persecution. He calls on Him to whom all hearts are known to witness that weak and ill as he is, he would undertake cheerfully any burden imposed on him by the Pope, were it to shed the last drop of his blood among the Saracens. When he approaches the grounds of his objection it is with an apology and a reiteration, 'I know and know of very truth that our Lord the Pope and the Holy Roman Church have this power that they freely dispose of all ecclesiastical benefices.' When he goes on, 'I know that whosoever abuses this power builds for hell-fire, and he does so abuse it who uses it not for the promotion of faith and charity,' he is leading up to the complaint that the patrons ought to be *asked* for their assent, ' maxime *quando de facili possit requiri.*' It is an abuse of power to override the patrons thus ; but

the *power* to do so is not denied, is indeed repeat-
edly asserted ('cum beneficia ecclesiastica aucto-
ritate potestiva conferantur'). It leads to scandal,
it puts Church dignitaries to confusion, it gives
a malicious satisfaction to their enemies, but it
cannot be denied or invalidated as a right. Even
when it upsets the appointment already made by
a bishop ('dictam praebendam contuli antequam
vestrae sanctitatis literas suscepissem'), it must be
borne, however grievous, 'non possum non ferre
moleste.' All that remains is to plead evidence of
past submissiveness, to promise future submission,
and meantime to beg that something may be done
to save one's face. 'I take leave to say that your
Holiness ought not, by thus conferring a prebend
in my Church without my sanction, to have put
to confusion one who is most obediently and
devotedly your humble servant, especially as I
always have been and always shall be prepared to
make liberal provision for any of your people to
much more than the value of that prebend, not
under compulsion to the confusion of myself or
the Church committed to me, but of my freewill
to the building up of charity.' We cannot even
say, 'Yes, but this was to an Englishman; had
it been not Master Acton the Legate's clerk, but
an Italian, a youth, a Papal nephew, it might have
been different;' for the very next clause in the
letter to Otto runs, 'Let me recall that since my
consecration to be bishop, a nephew of my Lord

the Pope has been promoted to one of the best prebends in the Church of Lincoln.'

' I beg therefore as a suppliant prostrate at the feet of your Holiness that you will in your benignity recall the collation to this prebend that I may not as a very abject from your love be unable for confusion to lift up my face before you and my brother bishops and my subject clergy.' To the mind of the writer resistance is not even conceivable. ' Rebellion is as the sin of witchcraft and refusal is as the iniquity of idolatry.' [1]

Apparently next year the Legate returned to the charge, but this time not by direct collation but by a request that Grosseteste would present Master Atto,[2] the Legate's clerk (no doubt the same man as the Acton of letter xlix), to a Lincoln prebend. This time the Bishop admitted Acton's qualifications as to learning and character, but offered three objections: (1) that to appoint him solely on the Legate's testimony was really acting on motives of fear or favour ; (2) that Acton himself had told the Bishop he had not got a dispensation to hold another benefice with cure of souls, and Grosseteste himself had resigned his own prior benefice on receiving a prebend because the Pope had told him the two could not be held together ; (3) that Acton was not quite suited to the post, well suited as he might be to others. Yet after all this, such is his conviction of the spiritual

[1] 1 Sam. xv. 23 (Vulgate).   [2] Letters, lxxiv.

motives, the wisdom and the goodness of the Papal
Legate, that he leaves the appointment absolutely
in his hands.   On hearing that the Legate is
offended with him for sending a messenger without
formal letters, he positively prostrates himself in
the dust before him.   The Legate's affection has
been to him warmth, life, and activity, the only
thing that has sustained him in his troubles and
prevented undue elation in prosperity ;   it has
brought him joy amid sorrows, consolation in
griefs, rescue from straits, relief from labours,
sweetness when all was bitter, light when all was
dark, union of hearts even at a distance, and
a perpetual call to perfection.[1]

This would seem pretty well to exhaust the
language of reverence and submission.   But even
a Legate is far below a Pope, and to the Pope
himself, ' kissing the blessed feet with utter submission and reverence,' he speaks of this submission
as due not only from all Christians, but from the
whole human race, and as the necessary condition
of attaining salvation.   The Pope has been set
like Jeremiah over all kingdoms, to root out and
to pull down, to build and to plant.   ' We owe to
you not merely our bounden duty but works of
supererogation over and above that. . . . If a monk
is to obey his superior even when he commands
what is impossible, how much more must we obey
every command of him who is in the place of

[1] Letters, civ.

Peter chief of the Apostles and of the whole world. . . . I deem all that I have to be more truly your property than my own.'

He is ' the gate at which whoso knocketh it shall be opened unto him ', ' the well of living waters from Lebanon ', 'the sure author of hopes and the refuge of all suppliants ', ' the church's consoler, rescuer, and shield, and the bridegroom who comes to wipe away her tears '.[1]   Nor is this mere diplomatic courtliness. The same language is used in explaining to the King that the Bishops had no option but to obey the Pope's orders for a tallage from all monks and clerks.

To the King he says, ' the Pope is our spiritual father and mother to whom we are incomparably more bound than to our parents in the flesh to honour and obey, revere and help him in every way. Were we to fail to help him now, we should be breaking God's commandment and our days will not be long in the land, we shall not be blessed in our children nor will our prayers be heard, we shall be heaping curses on our own heads, of all which things Holy Scripture gives manifest proof.'[2] For, once more, ' rebellion is as the sin of witch-craft.'

This is not the hyperbole of Oriental compliment where nothing would be so disconcerting as to have it acted on. If Grosseteste seems to strain language beyond its limits, it is because he actually feels he

[1] Letters, cxix.   [2] Letters, cix.

is speaking to God's actual vicegerent on earth, and in the expression of feeling about what is divine, human language—witness our hymns—has always toiled and panted in vain.

But one thing we may say, could the Grosseteste of this letter possibly be the writer of CXXVIII? Let alone that the inconsistency of opinions expressed within twelve years would be such that even a modern politician would boggle at it, we should have to make Grosseteste a man capable of using language which if not that of deep permanent conviction is nothing else than revolting.

Is the letter genuine?   On the other hand, ascribing the famous letter to Grosseteste is just like what a writer would do who was trying to affix the support of a great name to the broad general denunciation of Provisions. The facts of the particular case would not concern him; indeed, they would tend to narrow the issue. What he would want to put into currency would be an outspoken protest professing to come from the greatest English churchman of the time; one about whom there was already the rumour of his having openly rebuked the Pope and the Cardinals, and of his having by these rebukes goaded the Pope into most un-Pope-like language.

Forgeries common.   In this respect of putting the issue into a blunt and crude form and neglecting the local and temporary details, the letter is very like the many forged documents which skirmished about the edges of the great duel between Papacy and

Empire ; not forgeries in the ordinary sense, but academic exercises reminding one now of the speeches in Livy or Thucydides, now of a modern leading article. They are like seventeenth- and eighteenth-century pamphlets hitched on to some great name to sell them. For the ages when plagiarism was no crime because it was universal were also the ages when there was little critical sense in the ascription of authorship. Most work was either anonymous or not original. A few great names were apt to gather about them any floating productions. One only lends to the rich, and some such loans were thrust upon them without much heed to real appropriateness. The glaring inconsistencies of cxxvii are matched by others as glaring in documents circulated as from the pen of Frederick II. All are eagerly received by Matthew Paris, and in both cases from the same motive ; any stick will serve to beat a dog, and a zealous anti-Papalist may be in too great a hurry at the moment to inquire whether the name of Emperor is rightly or wrongly inscribed on one weapon, or the name of a famous churchman on the other.

When Grosseteste does meet a case that he feels he must reject, his rejections are not because the nominees are foreign, for often they are Englishmen as W. de Grana,[1] a boy still in his Ovid, or the kinsman of John Blundus,[2] the Chancellor of

Cases of actual rejection by Grosseteste.

---

[1] Letters, xvii.   [2] Ibid. xix.

York, whose examination paper is sent to the
Chancellor to show his kinsman's depth of illiteracy.
So the Legate Otto's clerk Acton [1] is an Englishman because otherwise the point would probably
be taken [2] in discussing his fitness on this later
occasion.

The Legate's nominee in another case [3] was
Thomas son of Earl Ferrers, who is objected to
as too young and not in orders. He begs the
Legate to persuade the Earl as patron to present
a more suitable person. Otherwise, seeing that
many things can lawfully be done by one of such
position as a Legate which a mere Bishop cannot
venture on, he waives his own standing in the
matter and leaves it wholly to the Legate's discretion, only reminding him that at the Day of
Judgement men will have to answer even for every
idle word. But he begs that a suitable vicar may
be appointed and that the young Thomas reside
regularly in the benefice, drawing part of the income
without cure of souls. This is interesting as
showing that even in a case flagrantly, as he says,
contravening both scripture and canon law, he
feels in the last resort he cannot resist an authority
derived from the Pope, but must be content with
the best safeguards he can provide. The next
case [4], that of the nephew of Master John the
Roman sub-dean of York, may very well be that

[1] Letters, xlix. M. Paris, iii. 419.   [2] Ibid. lxxiv.
[3] Ibid. lii.   [4] Ibid. lxxii.

of a foreigner. But he is rejected not for that, but as ' utterly illiterate ', so that the Bishop on his conscience dares not make the appointment, grateful as he is for much kindness received in the past from the sub-dean. In a last case [1] he does not reject, but cannot admit the presentee, simply because he himself has no adequate knowledge of him, and therefore hands it over to the archbishop, Boniface, who does know him, with the expression of a hope that he will consider more the good of souls than any one man's personal profit.

In five other cases the evidence shows that Cases of submis-neither would Grosseteste resist an appointment sion. simply on the ground of its being a nominee or relative of the Pope. His reference to his own appointment of a Papal nephew shows that he took pride in submitting his own judgement to the weight of an irresistible command, just as in CXVI he urges the Archbishop of York to do so. The Pope had charged him to impress on the Archbishop the duty of making a provision for the Bishop of Cervia, an exiled Papal partisan. ' We often have to do from obedience what we do with sorrow and would gladly leave undone if it might be so, for rebellion is as the sin of witchcraft.'

Nothing comes out more clearly than his deep Rebel-sense of the tremendous responsibility of the lion is as witch-Bishop who admits unfit presentees to the cure craft.

[1] Ibid. lxxxvii.

of souls. He must answer for each one of his sheep at the last great day. But still deeper is his sense of the duty of implicit obedience from all mankind to God's Vicar on earth. Even at the Judgement Day this plea will hold good, that he had yielded because rebellion is as the sin of witchcraft.

External evidence. It is one of a group of documents.

We must not isolate the letter, but read together the whole group of documents of which it forms a part. Such a one is Matthew Paris's story of the Pope's wrath, 'Who is this raving old man, as dotard as he is deaf, who has the audacity or rather the foolhardiness to sit in judgement thus ?' The Pope had a good mind to make him a byword and astonishment, an example and a portent to the whole world, or with a nod to ' our vassal, our slave the King of England ' have him thrown into prison. Then the Cardinals in a remarkable burst of candour point out that Grosseteste cannot be condemned, 'for what he says is true ; he is a man holier and of a more excellent way of life than we are. He has not his peer among prelates. The whole clergy of France and England know this. He is a great philosopher, a great scholar, famous as a lecturer, as a preacher, a lover of righteousness and purity, a persecutor of simony.' As their consciences thus pricked them, the Cardinals advised the Pope to bide his time ; the aged Bishop could not live long.

The letter and this remarkable story are bound together in Matthew Paris ; even if they do not

stand or fall together. We must not be too ready
arbitrarily to accept the letter and reject the
dialogue. The dialogue scene is at least *ben
trovato* ; which is more than can be said of the
style and composition of the letter.

Still more remarkable is the account of Grosse- Grosseteste's death-bed, which also comes in close con- teste's
death-
nexion with the preceding. The dying bishop is bed. The
hand is
made to castigate just the very things and persons the hand
of Mat-
that were the objects of Matthew Paris's perennial thew
Paris.
animosity, the violators of Magna Charta, the *non-
obstante* clause in Papal bulls, the usuries of Papal
money-lenders in England, the exaction of legacies
from the dying, the intrusion of unfit Papal presentees, the postponement of episcopal ordination.
He is made to denounce the Roman Curia as the
home of avarice, usury, simony, rapine, wanton-
ness, licentiousness, gluttony, and pomp ; to
denounce the king as its accomplice and sharer in
rapine ; and, most startling of all, to denounce the
Dominicans and Franciscans, for whom in his life
he had nothing but eulogy and the highest esteem.
These two orders he had held up as models, from
them he had drawn his best friends, and without
them he said his work would be impossible. Now
they are picked out as object-lessons in a fierce
indictment of heresy, for failing in their duty to
preach against Papal provisions ; and the Pope
himself becomes the arch-heretic. On this, Bishop
Stubbs is content to observe mildly that Grosse-

teste's view of the Papacy seems to have altered
at the end of his life.

It might have been at the same time observed
that the alteration was not only in his view of the
Papacy, but in his view of logic, his view of good
manners, even his view of Latin prose. But at any
rate we may with still greater caution put the
alternative that either Grosseteste's views altered
or else that those of Matthew Paris remained the
same and were put into Grosseteste's mouth.
Shall we still feel quite as comfortable in the
conclusion that ' the fact that Matthew Paris gives
the famous letter as Grosseteste's must remove any
doubt as to its genuineness ' ? Or do we not feel
even more ready to admit with the same editor
that ' it is somewhat remarkable that it is in none
of the MSS. which contain the collected letters
of Grosseteste ' ? [1]

Do con-
tempo-
raries
support
it ?

It may be said that even admitting Matthew
Paris was blinded by his own anti-Papal zeal on
the top of his natural tendency to the dramatic,
the cynical, and even the spicy, yet there must be
something in this readiness of the contemporaries
to believe in a bold anti-Papal declaration on
Grosseteste's part. The answer to this is twofold.
First, the wish was father to the thought. Those
who believed were only, among contemporary
authorities, the two whose personal and corporate
bias led strongly that way. There is no evidence

[1] Grosseteste, *Letters*, ed. Luard, p. xiii.

that other contemporaries believed. There is the
negative evidence that the more sober-minded did
not, or far greater sensation would have been
caused. There is the positive evidence that this Why was
letter was not inserted among Grosseteste's till it not in
a much later age. The first MS. of Grosseteste's lected
letters in which it is found is one of the fourteenth letters ?
century (Cambridge Public Library), and there is
in this no ascription to Grosseteste. In the Cotton
MS. of the letters of Adam Marsh, a MS. dating
from the early fourteenth century, it is written in
a later hand on the reverse of one page, but not
ascribed to Grosseteste. In the fourteenth century
there would be far less reluctance to repeat an
episcopal defiance of Rome. On the other hand,
Adam Marsh in a letter written within a year of
Grosseteste's death, refers to the ' imperterritam
illam responsionem . . . seculis omnibus profuturam'
which ' the bishop our Elijah ' wrote at the end of
his life ; but (1) Adam Marsh describes it as
written ' tam prudenter quam eloquenter et vehe-
menter ', of which three epithets the former two
hardly suit our letter, and (2) he speaks of it as
sent ' ad formidandam quam nostis maiestatem ',
which could hardly be said of ours. On the whole
it may be suggested as a solution that there were
several letters interchanged between Grosseteste
and the Pope on this case, ending in some sort of
protest. This was talked about and our letter
was drawn up purporting to be this protest, whereas

it is a flat refusal and obtained currency later as such.

Secondly, the over-readiness of some of the contemporaries to father upon Grosseteste an anti-Papal manifesto was connected with their similar greedy acceptance of malicious gossip about a rebuff supposed to have been administered to Grosseteste at the Papal court. He had gone to the Papal court in mid-Lent 1250, in his character of 'indefatigable persecutor of monks' (Matthew Paris, p. 96). They had appealed against him and 'cleverly bought protection from the Pope by cash down' (p. 97), '*pecunia interveniente*'. When he complained of his disappointment after all the promises he had received, the Pope, scowling at him, answers him, (p. 98) 'What business is it of yours? You have spoken your mind freely, and I have chosen to show them favour. Is thine eye evil because I am good?' The Bishop sighed, 'Oh, money, money, what a power thou art, especially in the court of Rome.' The Pope had overheard him and broke out angrily, 'You English are the most miserable of men. Each backbites the other and strives to reduce him to beggary. And you, how many of the monks subject to you, your fellow countrymen and of your own flock, whose heart is set on prayer and hospitality, are you draining of their resources that from their goods you may sate your own tyranny and greed and enrich others who are possibly aliens.' So the

Bishop retired in confusion, all calling shame on him, and to disguise his failure he turned to other business.

If this is true history, then Matthew Paris is indeed in luck. He could not have devised a situation more to his own mind. The persecutor of monks repulsed and rebuked before the highest tribunal, but getting in a shrewd side-thrust at Papal venality. This is to bring down two birds with one barrel. But is it true history or only the story dramatized gossip ? The Bishop certainly stayed very suspicious. on more than six months longer at Lyons, from the end of Lent to the end of September, though the other English prelates left Lyons nearly four months earlier. In a letter to Adam Marsh,[1] written, it seems, early in his stay at Lyons, his tone had been quite cheerful, and had led his friend to believe his business had prospered. That business was by no means confined, as Matthew Paris rather implies, to a struggle with the privileged monastic orders who had so many livings and whose privileges he wanted to revoke. He had other objects for his journey—to get support for his scheme of adequate endowment of vicarages, to vindicate the right to excommunicate a sheriff who would not back up the bishop's writ against an excommunicated clerk, and probably also to get protection for all English bishops from the claim of the Archbishop of Canterbury to exercise

[1] *Letters*, ed. Luard, lxxiii.

rights of visitation over them.   Incidentally it might be noted that dramatic propriety seems to fail a little in bringing a charge of cupidity against Grosseteste ; and in putting into the Pope's mouth a complaint of the enriching of foreigners. Moreover, it would be rather strange diplomacy to start off with the remark on venality quoted by Matthew Paris, especially when the utterer of the remark was still to spend six months of active business intercourse with those on whom it reflected.

The sermon at Lyons. The famous sermon itself [1] is attested by the evidence of the prefatory note by Robert Marsh, Archdeacon of Oxford, the one English Clerk who was present at his side.   It is still better attested by the intrinsic evidence of its style and tone, and by the fact that it is only a development of ideas and phrases which meet us again and again in his letters, such as the primacy of Moses and the parallel between the Pope's relation to the Church and that of a bishop to his diocese, the similitude from a pastor's duty to his sheep, and the familiar comparison of rebellion to witchcraft.   The peculiar phrase ' Deificatio ' and the argument built thereon, and the elaborate analogy of the arts may also be cited as characteristic.

And to put it beyond doubt, there is Adam Marsh's letter [2] of August 15, 1250, condoling with the Bishop on the unavailingness of his protest ;

[1] Browne, Fasciculus ii. 250–8.
[2] *Mon. Francisc.*, p. 153.

' they would not hear him because the Lord would slay them,' and comforting him by historical parallels beginning with Elijah, John the Baptist, the apostle Paul, the martyr Stephen, and other saints who withstood principalities and powers and spiritual wickedness in high places.

The sermon is a long document which must have taken a good hour to deliver. But its essential importance may be summed up under the following four heads :

(A) Its Papalism. It was a confidential address to the Pope and Cardinals alone, from one known to be the greatest living champion of the Papal theory. It never mentions the Papacy without the deepest reverence ; it is the book and school of the world, the throne of God, the sun of this sphere, the universal official saviour ; the Popes are clothed with the person of Christ, His representatives, His vicegerents, they are ' praesidentes in hac sacratissima sede sanctissimi Papae '. *Its Papalism.*

(B) Its theory of Anglicanism. He not only exalts the Papacy on theoretic grounds, but also because he sees in it the only hope for control, purification, and reform of the English Church. It is in England above all countries that the bishops' hands need strengthening, because in England above all countries the four enemies of bishops' authority are strong ; these four being the exempt abbeys, the royal prohibitions, the appeals to Rome, and the appeals to Canterbury *Its plea for the Bishops.*

and York. It was just for this he had come to
Lyons, to strengthen his hands as bishop against
monks and royal officers, and to check illusory
appeals. Far the greater part of the address is
taken up with the rights and duties of the episcopal
office, its divine appointment, its historic descent,
its difficulties, its transcendent importance and
responsibilities. And the Pope is not only the
first of bishops, but their power comes by way of
delegation from him ; he can delegate it to them,
but even he cannot diminish it or relinquish it.

Its sense   (C) Its sense of the pontificate of Innocent IV
of a crisis. as a crisis in Church history. So powerfully does
this weigh on his mind that it has forced him in fear
and trembling to speak out that he may not incur
the curse of the prophet, ' Woe unto him that is not
of clean lips.' And he does indeed speak out ;
' from the least to the greatest they are all given
to covetousness, from prophet unto priest, every
one dealeth falsely ; by reason of them men
blaspheme God's Name in every land ; they are
antichrists, robbers, betrayers of their sheep, men
who make the house of prayer into a den of
thieves. All this much and more is said of the
bad pastors.'

Its out-   (D) Its audacity. But what makes the address
spoken- unique among mediaeval documents are the pas-
ness. sages in which the blame for this is brought home
to the guilty parties :

     ' Of all this evil what is the prime and original cause ?

The cause, fountain-head, and origin of it is this court,
not only because it does not clear away these abomina-
tions as it alone can do, and as it is its bounden duty, but
because itself, by dispensations, provisions, and collations,
appoints these bad pastors, and so leads patrons to fill
benefices on carnal and worldly motives. The greater
the sinner's position, the greater is the sin. Let no one
say, this court in thus acting is acting for the behoof of
the Church as a whole. Woe unto them that say, " Let
us do evil that good may come." Again, let no one say
these pastors can appoint intermediaries ; these intermediaries also are bad. Nor does the pastoral charge
consist merely in administering the sacraments, chanting
the hours, celebrating masses, though rarely are even
these done properly by hirelings. It consists also in
teaching the truth, in overawing and chastising vice,
which hirelings have not the courage even if they had
the knowledge to do. It consists also in feeding the
hungry, clothing the naked, visiting the sick, and giving
hospitality. But these hirelings are only given enough
to support themselves. And all this is worse when parish
churches are appropriated by monastic bodies. This
most holy See is the throne of God, and the sun of the
world in His sight ; without which sun the world would
perish. Those who preside over this most holy See are
pre-eminent among mortals in being clothed with the
person of Christ, and obedience is due to them as to Him
in so far as they are true presidents. But if one of them,
which God forbid, put on the garment of love of kindred
or of the world, or of aught else but Christ, and thus act
against His precepts, he who obeys such a one manifestly
separates himself from Christ and from His body which
is the Church, and from the true presidency of this See ;
and if the whole world obeys such a one then hath come
the falling away and the son of perdition is at hand. God
forbid that this most holy See and those who preside in

it, whose orders the whole world obeys, should by ordering
aught contrary to the will of Christ be the cause of falling
away, or of schism among those who are one with God,
and will not do aught contrary to the will of Christ, who
hates nothing so much as the ruin of souls caused by
handing over the care of them to bad pastors.' ' It is
vain to plead the welfare of the Church as justification.'
' Those who strike with the sword shall perish with the
sword.' ' The whole world cries out against the unbridled
shamelessness of the familiars of this court '—' If the
Holy See do not speedily correct itself, destruction will
come upon it suddenly and it will be subjected to those
terrible things which God hath predicted by the mouth
of His Son and His holy prophets.'

The Pope's attitude to it.

The Pope who could allow an indictment like
this to be spoken to him was a strong and wise
man. It was characteristic of his cool, business-
like good sense that he saw it was better not to
burke the indictment, and that he made it easy
for the utterer of it to stay on six months in Lyons
after it and to carry his affairs to a successful
issue. Innocent would not be wholly displeased
to have his *familiares* thus made to feel their
unpopularity ; we see from the Papal register
that even an absolute ruler may often find it
difficult to keep his bureaucracy in hand. Not
once nor twice only he complains of the impor-
tunity of those around him, and of the measures
into which he had been hurried against his better
judgement. But there is a sound legal maxim
that a man is responsible for his agents ; and he
who wills the end wills the means.

There are few scenes in history so impressive
as this. The greatest scholar, writer, and churchman of his day delivering this appalling lecture to
one whom at the same time he salutes with emphatic
reiteration as God's vicegerent on earth. Never
does the essential theory of Papal omnipotence
stand out more clearly. It is a singular comment
which the great writer whom I have quoted has
made. According to Bishop Stubbs, it shows that Stubbs's
Grosseteste's view of the Papacy had changed. upon the
But the one bishop cannot forgive the other for scene.
making episcopal authority to be derived from
Papal. Between two such authorities, each a
famous Oxford Professor, each the leader of
European learning on several subjects, each the
head of this very diocese, it is hard to have to
choose. But if a choice must be made let it be
for Grosseteste. It would perhaps be unfair to
rest it on the accidental fact of his being Chancellor
of this University. But one other advantage he
has, on which it is not unfair to rest. He lived in
the thirteenth century ; and on the question what
view men of the thirteenth century took of the
Papal power, this fact may fairly count for something. If we still feel uneasy at finding ourselves on
a different side in an historical point to Dr. Stubbs,
we may fortify ourselves by remembering that on
the acceptance of canon law in England as authoritative we have to choose between him on one side
and a cloud of contemporary witnesses on the

other, including the three English canonists Athon,
De Burgh, and Lyndwood, for Stubbs's note
written in 1900 by way of answer to Maitland
cannot be said to alter the position, even though
it could almost be put on a half-sheet of note-paper;
or again, that on the moral and spiritual condition
of the English Church in the fifteenth century we
have once more to choose between him and contemporaries like Bishop Pecock and Gascoigne,
another Chancellor of this University.   If we are
wrong, we are wrong in good company on this
and perhaps on some other matters of Church
history on which the late Bishop of Oxford took
a pronounced line.

Was
Grosse-
teste's
visit to
Lyons a
failure,
as Mat-
thew
Paris
says ?

But the consequences of the scene as described
by Paris are a different matter.   The long stay
and great expenses of the Bishop at Lyons are
described as having ' failed to accomplish his
object ', he returns ' sad and empty-handed '.   He
thinks of resigning his See and retiring from a
world which is going to perdition, that he may give
his time to meditation, prayer, and study.   He
actually hands over the administration of the See
to Robert Marsh ; and is prevented from final
retirement only by the knowledge how the See
would be despoiled by the King during vacancy.
In the Lanercost Chronicle this becomes an actual
offer to resign made at Lyons ; and a passage in
one of his own letters (CXXX, p. 430) was interpreted
by Luard as referring to resignation.   But the

passage only says that he means to be up and doing, to ' break the bonds of wickedness ', but is at present not allowed to come ; probably, as Felten suggests, his doctor forbade it. How could the idea of resigning be read into a letter which prays that nothing may ever separate him from his flock and which breathes a very flame of energy for instant and radical reform ? ' Redeem the time . . . we know not when our Maker will take us hence.' ' He will require his people's blood at our hands . . . we must be up and doing.'

Besides, Adam Marsh's letter of August 15, while referring to Grosseteste's feeble health, expresses joy that Grosseteste does not mean to resign ; and his other letter of September 15, which could only have caught Grosseteste just as he was leaving Lyons, speaks of the ' opus Dei tam formidabile ' having been 'salubriter perseveratum' and brought to a ' triumphalis egressus '.

Matthew Paris's account then would have to be annotated severely. The Bishop returned much less ' sad ' than he had been till the latter part of his stay. His object was not the one object Matthew Paris suggests ; and he succeeded in this one, at any rate. He came back bent not on resignation, but on visitation ; and as to Robert Marsh, he had been the Bishop's *officiarius* as far back as 1248. There is nothing of the chronicler's baffled bishop, *tristis et vacuus*, about the Grosseteste who sent round to all his clergy the tremendous

letter cxxx which would dissipate in their minds
any such picture that rumour may have drawn
and keep them going from Michaelmas, the date of
his return, till after Christmas, when his health
allowed him to begin his visitations. There is
nothing of tension between him and the Papacy
in the action he took when leading the Bishops'
resistance to the Archbishops' usurpations. By
his advice the Bishops sent a proctor with 4,000
marks to resist Boniface. This sum, and the
Pope's being now out of the Savoyard sphere, are
in Matthew Paris's eyes the determining causes of
the decision going against the Archbishop. At any
rate Grosseteste, with his close ally Fulk Basset,
Bishop of London, were appointed conservators to
see that the whole series of Papal orders were
carried out. The whole case had taken from about
January 1251 to June 1252 ; during this time his
interest as spokesman of the English Church was
to keep from any cause of friction with the Papal
power. Yet it is just in and from this time that
Matthew Paris places the series of collisions with
that power which are made to reach their climax
in the famous letter of 1253. In speaking of the
good side of the Bishop's strictness in his diocese,
his purification of it, his forcing incumbents to
take orders, his preaching to priests and people,
the chronicler goes on to say ' he hated like
serpents' poison the wicked Romans who held the
Papal mandate that they should be provided for.

Grosse-
teste's
close re-
lations
with Pa-
pacy,
1250–3.

He used to say if he handed over to them the care of souls, he would be playing the Devil's part. Wherefore frequently he threw aside Papal bulls and flatly disobeyed such mandates '. It has now risen to ' frequently ', one should note.

Then in 1252 came the famous estimate attributed to Grosseteste that the revenues of the alien clerks put in by Innocent IV amounted to more than the 70,000 marks, while the net royal revenue was not one-third of that.

This estimate he had undertaken as he saw to what a pitch Roman avarice had mounted, as the Psalmist says, 'the presumption of them that hate thee increaseth ever more and more.' But the amount of 70,000 marks can hardly be anything but a monstrous over-estimate, as far as we can judge from the actual Papal Registers in the Vatican, and from the fact that Innocent IV himself in his letter of May 25, 1253, offered as a fair compromise a maximum of 8,000 marks a year, and 8,000 is not an arithmetical mean between 70,000 and 0. In Innocent's letter they assert it is more than 50,000 marks.'

It is probable that Innocent was aware of opposition from Grosseteste, and tried, as Mr. Stevenson suggests,[1] to overawe him by the unusually dictatorial tone of his letter of January 26, 1253. He would also have had time to hear Grosseteste's answer, which the Burton Annalist says was sent

[1] Stevenson's *R. Grosseteste*, p. 309.

straight to the Pope, though we need not any the
more assume that the violent letter we have was
the actual one written and sent. This may explain
the apologetic tone of the Papal letter of May 25,
1253, both excusing Provisions and limiting their
future amount and offering to compromise by
keeping down to 8,000 marks a year. The second
letter, November 3, 1253, was believed to be the
direct result of Grosseteste's letter, and thirty or
more copies of it were forwarded to the bishops
and chief abbeys of England ; it is a complete
restoration of the old rights of patronage to their
old owners. It may well be called by Matthew
Paris *aliquantulum mitigatoriae*,[1] and is put in its
sequence immediately after Innocent's mandate
and Grosseteste's defiance.

Matthew Paris unfair.

But in the actual history, Matthew Paris manages
to be unfair at once to Pope and Bishop.

Thus he is very unsatisfactory about the two
Papal letters of May 13 and November 3, 1253.
The latter he calls only *aliquantulum mitigatoriae*;
it is much more than that. The former he does
not give at all, but instead of it, under May 23,
1252,[2] a brief and vague declaration against Provisions in general, with no definite pledge of reform.
He is thus able to insinuate that Grosseteste's
action had no actual result, though his own

[1] M. Paris, vi. 260.
[2] Ibid. 210. The true date was May 1253, as the Papal
Registers show.

document [1] disproves his statement that nothing came of it but ' connivence and dissimulation ' on the Pope's part.

There is another letter, the last of this group of documents, which can with certainty be rejected as falsely ascribed to Grosseteste. For the letter violates all Grosseteste's principles by appealing to the secular power for armed interference in an ecclesiastical affair, by aiming at the total exclusion of all Provisions and even of suits in the Papal court, by laying stress on the pecuniary aspect of the matter. It is too crude and awkward in style and argument, too rough in tone, and too insular in its patriotism, to be mistaken for his by any one who has read the genuine letters of a man who was intensely sacerdotal and Papalist, spiritual-minded, uninsular, a writer always dignified, polished, and profound.

Matthew Paris's account of the visit to Lyons in 1250 is, as I have indicated, quite inconsistent with Grosseteste's lifelong convictions as to the *pleni-tudo potestatis* of the Papacy. It is also quite inconsistent with the Pope's treatment of him. He was evidently regarded, and regarded himself, as carrying great weight at the Papal court. He was on intimate terms with at least four of the Cardinals (Otto, Giles, Thomas, Raynald), and six of the high officials (Ernulfus penitentiary, Ranfrid notary, John of Ferentino a chamberlain, Martin

Grosseteste's influence at the Papal Court.

<hr>

[1] M. Paris, v. 393.

a chamberlain, and the friars Elias of Cortona and
Raymond of Pennaforte). As long as he lived under
Innocent IV he was receiving important bulls from
the Papal chancery. One of the first bulls issued
by the new Pope (August 8, 1254) was in his favour,
and a sharp rebuke to the extravagant behaviour
of the monks of Christ Church, Canterbury.

The great suit between him and his chapter was
decided in his favour by a bull of August 25, 1245.
The struggle between him and the monks of his
diocese was decided, largely at least in his favour,
by a bull of September 25, 1250, allowing him to
institute adequate vicarages at the expense of
monastic impropriators ; a bull which Matthew
Paris himself quotes, though it destroys his claim
of a monastic victory over the Bishop, and though
he has a parting shaft at the Bishop's action as
' more to spite the monks than to assist the vicars '.

Other
stories.
Finally a dramatic close was given to the whole
story by the growth of the legend that Grosseteste
was excommunicated for his action. This legend
first appears in the Lanercost Chronicle, and is
enlarged by the later writers ; ' he appealed to the
most high Judge.' It grew out of the Matthew
Paris story of Grosseteste's being suspended in
1251. But there is no evidence at all for it, and
there is direct evidence against it.

The question of the authenticity of Grosseteste's
two letters to the Pope and to the English laity,
and his death-bed utterances, whichever way

decided, still leaves us able to state some general conclusions. These are :

(1) The vast potentialities of the Papacy during the period covered by the greater part of these letters, i.e. from 1230 to 1245. It had a deeper and truer hold on England than on any part of Christendom. Its services during the years of trouble 1216–19 were gratefully remembered, and the evil days of Provisions had hardly yet begun.

(2) The intense conviction of the best minds of the age that on the connexion with Rome depended the security of the national Church as against the secular power, the internal discipline and purity of that Church, and the whole prospect of further reform. Only when he finds his trust in Rome to be a broken reed does Grosseteste's heart fail him awhile, and then his disappointment is so great that he is thrown into absolute despair.

(3) The width and depth of the havoc wrought in this position by Innocent IV. The very crudity of the views for which the popular resentment sought to make a mouthpiece and champion of Grosseteste is eloquent of the mischief wrought by Innocent IV in eleven and a half years of ' warring solely with spiritual weapons '.

(4) The one-sidedness and the violence, the suppressions and the exaggerations, of Matthew Paris. He is our chief authority for the period, and so is indispensable. His dramatic talent, his outspoken boldness, his appeal to English

prejudices of the most rooted kind, have combined
to make him irresistible.   Obviously, too, he takes
a keen interest in seeking information, and often
has access to documents and informants of the
first rank.   Yet with all this he is often utterly
untrustworthy.

This constitutes a serious difficulty.   We have
been accustomed to go to him as to a fountain-head,
but, as Aristotle says, ὅταν τὸ ὕδωρ πνίγῃ, τί δεῖ ἐπιπίνειν;

Medi-
aeval
unity ;
modern
disunion.

The united action of the civilized world in
pursuit of the highest aims which it could con-
ceive ; this was the dominant thought in Grosseteste's mind ; it is a thought strange enough to
modern minds.   We have swung over to the
opposite pole, and accept disunion of the most
complete kind in religious beliefs, in political aims,
even in industrial pursuits.   But is it not possible
that we may have reached an extreme in this
direction ? or, to vary the metaphor, may not the
wheel be now at its lowest point ; may it not be
about to begin, even now, to mount slowly up
again ?   One of the great facts of the last fifty
years has been that tendency to aggregation of
scattered fragments into larger political units
which we know under the name of nationalism ;
the union of Germany, the union of Italy, perhaps
the movement towards a pan-Slavonic union.   Nor
are Brussels conventions and Hague conferences
without some significance in this direction.   At
any rate we need not assume that anarchy and

disruption are things good in themselves, or that to profess a religion which we do not really intend to translate directly into practice is better than the impetuous idealism of the Middle Ages, failure as that was. There are some failures which are greater than success.

The modern English acquiescence in the anomalous, the chaotic, the illogical, is more modern than is sometimes supposed. It is due partly to the Protestant and Puritan trend impressed by historic events upon our religious development, partly to the piecemeal and rebellious character of the development of our constitution ; partly to mere insularity and isolation from the main currents of the European stream. But we must not expect to fit mediaeval England into this Procrustean bed. Still less must we assume that mediaeval England is irrational for not conforming to this set of beliefs.

We may fairly be asked to extend to mediaeval religion, mediaeval politics, mediaeval law, some of that justice which is beginning to be extended to mediaeval art and mediaeval literature. At any rate it can fairly be asked and even demanded of us that we do not misread their history by reading it through our own prejudices.

Christendom was destined to break up into the nations of Europe. If any one says that this disruption was all for the best—that what had to be is that which ought to be—I would not quarrel with what I cannot presume either to affirm or to

Need the Reformation have come just in the way it did ?

deny. But if we reflect on the beauty, the majesty, the potentialities of that which the word 'Christendom' embodied; if we realize that the conception of a reign of God upon earth was the ideal to which men did homage in their hearts—however much their conduct fell short of their ideal, as conduct now falls short and will do in all ages—if, moreover, we weigh and measure by what cruel blows, by what wanton disillusioning, they were forced to loosen their clinging hold and even to ask in stupefaction the question whether God's Vicar could be doing Satan's work, whether he could be the Antichrist, then we may turn and meet the problem whether it has been for the good of mankind that the Reformation which had to come should come as a revolution, that the Church of saints and martyrs, of missioners and crusaders, should be dragged through the mire of Avignon and bound to the chariot wheels of contemptible Italian dynasties, should become 'an example of all the shames and infamies in the world ', as one of its greatest servants called it ?

Has it made for righteousness that every schoolboy, as Macaulay would say, is prepared to treat Papal history as the storehouse of instances of hypocrisy and avarice, immorality, and nepotism; that to the average man it is the monumental warning—a superfluous warning indeed—not to profess virtue in politics or worldly business ?

Have we as a nation lost nothing by our recoil

from the mediaeval attempt to interpenetrate daily
life with religion, to set a standard by counsels of
perfection, to organize and centralize the agencies
of good ?

In short, has not Grosseteste's view an interest
in itself for us, if only by contrast with our own
view, as well as an historic importance as giving
the key to his age ?

PROTESTS AGAINST PAPAL ABUSES, 1245–1254
MATTHEW PARIS

The cru-
cial years
1245–54.
THE movement against the Papacy, or rather against certain measures of the Papacy, goes back, as we saw, to the Berkshire rectors' protest in 1240,[1] or even earlier. But it is under Innocent IV, and especially after the Council of Lyons, that the movement becomes continuous and increasing. The crucial years, therefore, are from 1245 to 1254. Before him, it had taken the form chiefly of discontent at Papal taxation of the Church. The taxation had become constant, and it was to make war on an Emperor for whom up to 1245 there was sympathy felt in England even by the clergy,[2] rather than much reprobation. But by itself taxation, even taxation in novel forms or abnormal amount, would not have produced more than the usual struggles to escape. And after 1245 the war was on an Emperor against whom the voice of the Church had gone forth, and his manifestoes to secular princes had turned the clergy everywhere against him. Taxation therefore would hardly have led to revolt. But Innocent IV gave an immense acceleration and bitterness to the movement by

[1] *Ann. Monast.* (Burton), i. 265.
[2] M. Paris, iv. 307.

his Provisions. This comes out in the two letters sent to him in 1246, from the English clergy and the English barons.[1]

The English envoys, William Powic and Henry de la Mare, had been sent from the Parliament which met March 18, 1246, at London,[2] to complain that Innocent IV had promised, at Lyons, not to exceed twelve Provisions ; to leave bishops and lay patrons their patronage ; to provide for English clerks and to dispense for pluralities in case of highborn and reputable persons, and *ne Italicus Italico immediate succedat.* In return for these promises the English prelates at Lyons had agreed to a tax on English clergy for the succour of Constantinople, a tax ranging from one-half on non-residents, to one-third on others, and one-twentieth on the poorest.

The English grievances.

But the English grievances presented at Lyons [3] had been Provisions ('60,000 marks a year', it was said), the powers exercised by Master Martin, the *Non Obstante* clause, and King John's tribute. Their memorial of these grievances had been put aside, and hardly touched by the general statutes

---

[1] They are given fully and well in Matthew Paris, iv. 526, &c., 580, &c. ; in a shorter and more confused form in the *Annals of Burton*, pp. 278–85, in which the general grievances of the Parliament are tacked on to the barons' letter, and the December letter of the clergy tacked on to the letter sent by the abbots and priors in March.

[2] *Ann. Monast.* (Burton), iii. 169 ; M. Paris, iv. 518.

[3] M. Paris, iv. 441–4.

of the Council ; and they had left, vowing to refuse the annual tribute and other ecclesiastical taxation ; and Henry III had angrily backed up this, according to Matthew Paris,[1] though with characteristic mediaeval tolerance of contradictories. The King's remarkable words to Grosseteste [2] show it was quite compatible with absolute loyalty to the theory of Papacy—another warning against the modern tendency to read history backwards, and so to read too much ' Protestant Reformation ' into these protests.

So in the letters of expostulation sent by the bishops and the abbots, there is the most humble acknowledgement of the Pope's supremacy ; ' they long with their whole mind and heart to be found ever more and more fervent in devotion to the Holy See ; it is the pillar of the Church, set up by God and not by man ; they appeal to it with prayers and tears.' [3] Even the barons write 'imploring in all humbleness and devotion '.[4] The King writes as a loving son, which he means always to be to the mother who nursed him at her breast.[5]

---

[1] M. Paris, iv. 479.

[2] Grosseteste, *Epist.* 338–9. Cp. M. Paris, iv. 528–35. He promises devotion and obedience to the Holy See as his spiritual mother ; the day he ever fails in this ' damus oculum ad eruendum immo caput ad amputandum. Praeter communes rationes quibus omnes Christiani principes tenentur ecclesiae, nos . . . arctius obligamur . . .' The Holy See had saved his throne.   [3] M. Paris, iv. 530.

[4] Ibid. 533.   [5] Ibid. 535.

But each letter closes with more than a hint of the seriousness of the crisis. The bishops say they cannot restrain the national feeling. The abbots predict disturbance, scandal and schism, and a split between the *regnum* and the *sacerdotium*. The barons say they will have to 'set up a wall to protect the house of God and the liberty of the kingdom'. The King speaks of the danger of an irreparable blow both to the royal power and to the Papal authority.

But meantime Papal orders were going out (March 24) for the collection of the one-twentieth already demanded at Lyons ; and a new Papal claim [1] to the goods of intestate clerks had been raised. The King rejected the latter claim, and forbade the bishops to proceed with the former on pain of losing their baronies. 'Thus the English Church was between the upper and the nether millstones, between Scylla and Charybdis.' [2]

When, therefore, the Pope was able to beat down contemptuously all this opposition by the mere rumour that he was prepared to issue an interdict,[3] the *plenitudo potestatis* appeared in all its irresistibleness. But the vital point, Provisions, had not been touched. There was even a belief that the Pope was willing henceforth to issue no Provisions without the King's consent.[4] Certainly the Papal registers [5] for 1246, and down to March 1247, The Pope inflexible.

---

[1] M. Paris, iv. 552.   [2] Ibid. 559.   [3] Ibid. 561.
[4] Rymer, i. 266.   [5] Nos. 2481 and 1672.

contain only *one* provision for a foreigner (Matthew
of Alperno, Papal chaplain, and that with a sort
of apology, that he had lost his suit against Philip
de Lucy for the Church of Overton in Winchester
diocese ; Philip being a clerk of Earl Richard of
Cornwall). The last in favour of a foreigner before
that had been October 19, 1245, in favour of
a Papal chaplain who held a canonry at Hereford.

Also just in this summer of 1246 a great concession to English prelates was promised, to the
effect *ne Italicus Italico succedat.* But most of
the struggle during 1246 was concentrated on the
subject of Papal taxation of the Clergy.

The envoys, William Powic and Henry de la
Mare, had reported to the Winchester Parliament,
June 7, 1246, that the Pope had only repulsed
them, saying, ' The King of England is now kicking
against the pricks, siding with Frederick (*recal-
citrat et Fretherizat*) ;[1] he has his plan, I have
mine, which also I mean to follow.' The King's
answer at first was to forbid all collection of the
tax.[2] The Pope in return threatened the prelates
with excommunication and suspension if it was not
paid in to his agent by Ascensiontide, August 15.
But the bishops who had been entrusted with the
interdict reasoned with the King, so did his brother
Earl Richard, who had some secret understanding
with the Papacy that made him its eager supporter.
The King was cowed and gave way, and ' the whole

---

[1] M. Paris, iv. 560.   [2] Ibid. 558.

great effort made by magnates and bishops and the hope of liberating the kingdom and the Church of England were miserably and cruelly foiled '.[1] Benefices under 100 marks had to pay one-twentieth ; those over 100, one-third, or non-residents, one-half ; *non obstante* any previous privileges, ' the most detestable clause of all.' [2] This once more roused the King to prohibit the Bishop of London from beginning the collection ; and getting what comfort they could from this flicker of resolution on the part of the King, the clergy on December 1 drew up a formal protest. They estimate that the tax would amount to 80,000 marks, a sum beyond the power of all England to pay ; for to raise Richard I's ransom of 60,000, the churches had had to sacrifice their crosses and chalices. It would so impoverish canons that they would be unable to keep residence, and monks so that they would be unable to sustain the poor ; parish priests would have to drop their services ; the countless poor will take to robbery. The clergy therefore Protest unite in a refusal in the Name of Our Lord, and by the clergy; appeal to a General Council.[3]

The magnitude of the sum may be exaggerated. We can never trust mediaeval figures even when they are given with the greatest definiteness, and it was a clerical statistician who repeated at the Council of Constance the monstrous misstatement that the number of parishes in England was 45,000.

[1] M. Paris, iv. 561.   [2] Ibid. 580.   [3] Ibid. 583.

Mediaeval men were also, even more than modern,
infected with an ignorant impatience of taxation.
Still there can be no question as to the seriousness
of this appeal to a General Council. It was the one
weak joint in the armour of Papal power. The
most loyal clergy in Christendom [1] had at last been
its bear- forced into a position that must sooner or later
ing on
the undermine the theory itself. They would disguise
theory
of Papal it from themselves as long as they could, but it
suprem- is impossible even in the Middle Ages to go on
acy.
indefinitely accepting a theory and rejecting it in
practice. The practice must in time react upon the
theory. That it took so long to do so, that in the
thirteenth and fourteenth centuries English canonists would still lay down that rebellion is as the
sin of witchcraft, this only proves the ineradicable
hold the theory had upon their minds. It held
them by what was best and strongest in them,
and it remained even after they had been forced
into a protest that looks to us, but was not to
them, a denial of the theory itself. Vassals could
only protest against feudal tyranny by a temporary
' defiance ' ; ecclesiastics could only protest against
Papal tyranny by appeal to a Council. But the
feudal bond still remained the highest expression of social duty, and the Bishop of Rome
still remained the successor of Peter and the
rock on which the Church was built. Nearly

---

[1] M. Paris, iv. 530 ' regnum sacrosanctae Romanae ecclesiae
specialiter devotum.'

two centuries were to elapse before it could be said, every other man you meet is a Lollard. But Innocent IV, by the end of 1246, had effected the first stage in this long process.

In 1246 the laity had naturally been more out- The pro-
spoken even than the clergy, as we have seen. The test by
St.Louis.
laity of France could take the strongest ground of all, as it was Louis himself [1] who presented the gravamina of the Church and nation. He, as ' rex Christianissimus and a devout Son of the Church ', had kept back his feelings in the hope that there would be some redress in answer to complaints. The nation was united on these points: they were amazed he had borne it so long, and they were not only fast losing that devotion they used to have for Rome, but already it was nearly extinct, and even worse, turned to violent hate and violent bitterness, a hatred which, as all Christians must fear, will produce some terrible and portentous result. If these things be done in the green tree, what would be done in the dry ? What would happen in other countries, if this had happened in France which had been so devoted ? The only thing which was keeping the laity in obedience was the royal power. ' As to the clergy, God knows, and many men know too, with what feelings they sustain this yoke. And if the cause be asked whereby this offence cometh, it is this, my Lord,

[1] In May 1247 ; laity in June 1247. M. Paris, vi. (Addita-menta) 99–112.

I take leave to say to you, that you are bringing new things upon the earth ; things which are of a truth new, and hitherto unheard of.' Such things were the tax on temporalities of the Gallican Church ; the use of the threat, Pay me such-and-such a sum or I will excommunicate you ; the treatment by Papal nuncios of the highest Church dignitaries as if they were serfs or Jews. It was the Papal nuncio, the Bishop of Palestrina, who first devised the plan of calling up a bishop or abbot and saying to him: 'If you reveal by word or writing, by act or sign, what I am about to say to you, you are *ipso facto* excommunicated;' and then when he had thus sealed his lips, going on : ' I order you to pay so much for the Pope on pain of excommunication.' It was not to be believed that the Pope knew all the oppressions practised by his envoys. But the Pope himself conferred multitudes of provisions and pensions, he conferred prebends and parsonages before they were vacant— a thing never done before, and prohibited by the law.

' Now, though you are not bound by human law, yet it is seemly that you should bind yourself by the law you yourself have made, as even our Lord Jesus Christ submitted to the laws. It is a horrid sight in God's church, that the living canons should daily be face to face with those who are waiting for them to die, like crows waiting for corpses. The *plenitudo potestatis* enables you to do these things, but its exercise ought to be kept in bounds by reason and moderation. The Holy See has

the primacy, and doubtful questions ought to be referred
to it, but we do not read in Scripture, in canon law or in
history, that it ought to despoil other Sees.

' Pope Alexander III took refuge in France, but did not
lay burdens on the Gallican Church. Pope Paschal took
refuge in France, but did none of the things that were
being done now. Pope Gelasius took refuge in France,
and Calixtus II was a Frenchman, but they laid no
burdens on the Gallican Church. Innocent II took refuge
in France, but he laid no burden on the Gallican Church.
It might be said that they could have done what is being
done now, but did not choose to do it ; to which the
answer is, " We grant your power as theirs, only let your
use of it be as theirs." Assuredly if it was not expedient
to do it then, it is less expedient now, when all Christendom is in far greater disturbance. And pray God the
disturbance do not increase ; for he who squeezes too hard,
draws blood." But all your predecessors together, it is
said, did not confer so many as you alone have done in this
brief time. Gradually your power has increased to its
present boundless extent. . . . These foreigners do not
reside ; they are mere names, perhaps sham names, under
cover of which churches and patrons are plundered. All
that the Church of Rome gets is the scandal and the hatred
and the loss of her subjects' devotion. Finally the king
informs you of what you know as a fact, that he loves you
with sincere affection, and deeply sympathizes with your
necessities ; but all that cannot make him neglect the
liberties and constitution of the kingdom entrusted to
him by God. . . . He therefore begs you affectionately as
his very dear father in Christ, and he earnestly seeks of
you for the honour of God, of yourself, and of the Church,
. . . to spare the churches henceforth, to cease from these
acts and to revoke the latest of them.'

Here we have four times repeated the acknowledgement that knocks the bottom out of all

Its re-
peated
acknow-
ledge-
ment of
the *pleni-
tudo po-
testatis.*

resistance, however justifiable, however eloquent. It is acknowledged that the Pope is above law, that he has the *plenitudo potestatis* ; that his See holds the primacy, that he can act as he chooses. Then there can be no talk of real resistance in the end ; it can only at highest be expostulation, or no more than humble entreaty. This is why there will be centuries of continued and growing abuses, why the intolerable will be tolerated, why frauds and scandals seen clearly enough will yet be submitted to ; why grievances will futilely tread the same bewitched circle from this Parliament of Paris to the Council of Constance, or even to the Diet of Worms. The mighty theory of God upon earth once accepted, all its consequences must be accepted too. To Wiclif in the fourteenth century the Pope may be 'a sinful caitiff, perchance a damned fiend ' ; a hundred years earlier even Grosseteste could allow the position to be put that the Pope might be a heretic;[1] but his power is of God, and common men have not to judge, but only to obey. The only way out of the circle is to break in upon the theory itself, and this no one was yet ready to do.

Hence the Pope has only to be firm, and opposition must soon be intimidated. If it is he who gives way, there must be special circumstances to explain it.

The whole letter of St. Louis is interesting from

[1] M. Paris, v. 402.

the depth of religious feeling displayed in it. The
issue was one which evoked this, as well as other
lower feelings of human nature. Jealousy of
foreigners as such, and tenacity in proprietorship
of church patronage are strong and natural, if not
lofty motives. But St. Louis elevates the discus-
sion by his genuine zeal for the ancient loyalty to
Rome. In fact the document is so characteristic of
him in its mingling of simplicity and shrewdness,
candour and discretion, even business and religion,
that this alone might stamp it as genuine. It is Its date.
wrongly referred to 1245 by Matthew Paris and by
his editor in the Rolls Series. The allusions in
it evidently belong to the circumstances of 1247,[1]
not 1245 ; and it is evidently later than the first
appeal sent May 2, 1247, as we know by a confidential letter from Archbishop Boniface to his
brother Peter of Savoy.[2] In substance it is much
the same as the appeals sent a few months earlier
from England, though it is couched in a more
stately form. The chief stress is laid on the
unprecedented character of the Papal taxation, and
particularly on the abuse of Provisions. It cannot
be read without producing a conviction that
Innocent IV's pontificate made a new and disastrous epoch in European history *parere aliquid
grande monstrum.*

The silence of the French chronicles perhaps

---

[1] Berger, St. Louis et Innocent IV, 270, &c.
[2] M. Paris, vi. 131-3.

indicates Louis's wish to keep it comparatively
private; for as he says, he has hitherto not made
formal complaints (*dissimulavit et siluit*), but only
entreaties (*preces*). Its appearance in Matthew
Paris's pages may mean that a copy of it was
sent officially by Louis to his brother-sovereign in
England to keep him in touch with what was
being done. Or Matthew Paris may have got
a copy from Lyons through his correspondents
there; he had already got the letter sent from
Lyons early in May 1247 by Boniface of Savoy to
his brother Peter of Savoy, on the previous French
demands. This letter must have come to Matthew
Paris through an English channel; so perhaps we
may guess the French king's of June 1247 did too,
though it came later, to judge by the documents
among which it is placed. The date assigned to
it, 1245, was only an after-thought of Matthew
Paris, adding as a pencil-note at the foot of the
page, 'Letter presented at Council of Lyons on
oppressions of the Church.' If he had brought it
a moment into comparison with the May letter
from Boniface, or with the events of 1245 and
1247 respectively, he would have seen its date
must be not 1245 but June 1247, as it must come
between Innocent IV's announcement, May 30, to
the Archbishop of Narbonne that the Emperor was
going to march on Lyons, and St. Louis's promise
in mid-June to defend the Pope if attacked.

Its auth-
enticity.　　The authenticity of the document is patent on

the face of it. It is borne out as to the abuse of
procurations by the words of Thomas of Cantimpre;
the Papal envoys came, he says, ' cum magnis
exercitibus potius quam familiis,' by the same
complaints at Metz, Nîmes, Albi, Cahors, and
other places, and by the Pope's concessions on the
matter, which were hastily granted June 12, 1247,
reducing the scale in Narbonne to that of other
provinces.[1] It is also borne out as to recent Papal
taxation by the Verdun chronicler : ' One-tenth
of clerical revenue was taken at this time to supply
the Pope with soldiery . . . as much as £1,000 in
all was taken from the church of Verdun.' The
other counts in the indictment are more than
borne out by the Papal registers. These show the
main abuse of Provisions, going back to Celes-
tine III, not, as King Louis thought, begun by
Innocent III ; but it is true that, though common
under Innocent III, they increase enormously
under Innocent IV, so that it becomes a very
usual safeguard to procure a clause exempting
from liability to make Provision, unless this clause
be specially cited. Often they are granted to
minors under nineteen (nos. 5191, 7224), even
minors under eighteen (no. 376) ; in the greater
number of cases, however, the age is unspecified.
Blank forms are obtained by Prelates allowing
them to dispense in two, four, or six cases, or even
up to forty (no. 4003). The grants often imply

Evidence of the Registers.

[1] Register, 2784, 3969 ; Potthast, 117, 126.

absenteeism and pluralities despite the strict rules on these heads passed by the Lateran council of 1215, which said that dispensation from the rules was only to be in the case of persons eminent for rank or for learning. The University of Paris in 1258 laid down that a pluralist could not hope to be saved;[1] and Gregory IX was believed to have said that the Pope could not dispense for pluralities. Some of Innocent IV's cases were no doubt cases of benefices too small in salary to go alone (nos. 2048, 4834); and others were cases of leave of absence for study (nos. 1914, 2270). But the fact remains that the whole system grew under him to monstrous proportions. Even he felt it was not decent, and might be dangerous, to continue the pressure on France during the Crusade; so the French cases decline 1248–50, but rise again after the Emperor's death gave the Pope a free hand once more. At the very opening of his pontificate his nephew Ottobono had been provided as chancellor of Reims, and archdeacon of Parma; in 1248 he and three Papal great-nephews are given a sweeping dispensation from the rules against pluralities (no. 3935). Preferments, pensions, or dispensations, follow rapidly for Papal chaplains, Gerard of Parma, John of Vercelli, Adenolfo, nephew of the late Pope; Papal writers, Philip of Assisi, Jacopo of Bevagna, Master Rostand, Master Berard of Naples, Henry of Milan,

[1] Berger, St. Louis, p. 288 [2].

Albert of Incisa ; and many others in the service of favoured cardinals.

Sinibald and Tedisio Fieschi, and Bernard of Foliano, nephews of the Pope, hold canonries at Rouen and at Beauvais and at Tours. John of Camezano, another nephew, held a French, an English, and a Flemish canonry simultaneously. Master Stephen, Papal subdeacon and chaplain, nephew of the cardinal of SS. Cosmo and Damian, held twelve benefices in Spain, four in France, one in Bohemia (no. 6044).

Behind these we can discern less presentable figures many in number. Yet the pressure on France was as nothing to that on England, and there was a good deal of care taken to avoid the central part of the kingdom and the royal domain. Also the protests of Louis were listened to, while those of Henry were not.

In England it was patriotically believed that John Tolet, the one English Cardinal, tried to reason with the Pope by pointing out how evil the times were ; the Holy Land in danger, the Greek Church estranged, the hostility of the Emperor, the imminent destruction of Hungary by the Tartars, the civil war in Germany, the Spaniards incensed against the clergy, France in revolt, and England, like Balaam's ass, after being spurred and beaten, at length finding voice ; ' We [the Papal court] are like Ishmael, every man's hand is against us and all hate us.' [1]

[1] M. Paris, iv. 579.

Compari-
son be-
tween
England
and
France. The chief difference in the position, as it developed in France and in England respectively, lay in the circumstances and the character of the two kings. Louis had to be handled with far more respect by a Pope who was a refugee within the sphere of French influence. It was of vital importance to conciliate him, already far the most respected figure in Europe, the friend still and ally of the Emperor, a man not made of the malleable stuff of Henry III. The English King was technically the Pope's vassal. At any moment he was capable of being caught by a baited hook, as Matthew Paris puts it. Already in 1246, both July[1] and December,[2] it was rumoured in England that for all his passionate outbursts he was preparing to climb down from his heroics, and was ready to desert the cause if the Pope would only enable him too in his turn to squeeze subsidies from the English clergy. A chronic bankrupt cannot afford the unremunerative virtue of constancy.

Thus a few ' shadowy ' concessions,[3] that Provisions shall be notified to the King for approval, that the proposal about intestates is recalled, were enough to give Henry the excuse he wanted for desertion. ' For what did it matter to the venal notaries of the Curia, that they had formally to request the King to enrich them and impoverish himself at an order from the Pope ? '

---

[1] M. Paris, iv. 559, 561.   [2] Ibid. 577, 579.

[3] Ibid. 550, 598, 604.

The Pope knew what manner of man he had to
deal with, and remained quite firm in regard to
the tax from the clergy of one-twentieth, one-
third, and one-half. He also by steady pressure
got in the annual tribute of 1,000 marks ; by the
close of 1249 the tribute was only half a year in
arrear.[1] He even appointed new collectors,[2] two
English Franciscans—ravening wolves in sheep's
clothing, Matthew Paris calls them. They were
armed with 'thundering' Papal bulls, and travelled
about on excellent nags, with boots and spurs,
' a scandal to their order.' They began by demand-
ing 6,000 marks from the See of Lincoln, to the
' stupefaction ' of the Bishop, and 400 marks from
the Abbey of St. Albans. The monks made a
gallant struggle for more than a year, but their
prior, aged as he was, had to journey to Lyons,
and then they only compromised for 200 marks,
besides 100 more in expenses. Once more, in the New
English
spring of 1247,[3] the clergy and laity sent their protests.
joint remonstrances both to the Pope and the
cardinals. To the former they dwelt on the im-
memorial zeal of the Church of England on behalf
of its mother the holy Roman Church, to which it
gave service devotedly, and ' never means to
recede from its allegiance, to which it owes all
its moral progress (*per incrementa morum semper*

[1] Rymer, i. 271.
[2] M. Paris, iv. 617–22, and vi. (Additamenta) 119.
[3] Ibid. iv. 595.

proficiens). Now kneeling at the feet of your
Holiness, we earnestly beseech you in pity to spare
us the demand for money, a demand that we
cannot bear, that is beyond our power ; for our
country though rich in produce is poor in cash.
We are also ordered by your Holiness to contribute
to the King ; we cannot in honour fail him at his
need, nor ought we to fail him. The bearers will
explain to you the disastrous consequences which
threaten from an impost we cannot possibly
endure, bound as we are to you by every tie of
love, obedience, and devotion '. This hint at the
end is couched more plainly in the letter to the
cardinals. The various taxes paid by the clergy
to Papal order since 1216 are enumerated. The
present tax will go partly to help the French,
the enemies of England, to reconquer the Greek
Empire ; partly to help the Holy Land, which
could be better recovered in other ways ; partly
to other aims of the Pope. The total sum demanded could not be raised even if the whole
property of the clergy was sold up. The college
is begged to take such steps as will prevent the
estrangement of devout sons of the Church, and
restore them to her bosom and to their old obedience. The marginal note[1] opposite these last words
runs : ' Note here a word of dread, the hidden
threat of desertion from the obedience of Rome.'
But all was in vain. The prelates themselves gave

[1] M. Paris, iv. 597, note.

way, and it was rumoured that the King had entered on a collusive arrangement with the Pope.[1] The year 1247 had produced an increased bitterness against both. The next year, 1248, added a new grievance in the extraordinary powers conferred by the Pope on the Archbishop of Canterbury,[2] who was allowed to take a year's revenues of all churches vacant within the province, till the sum of 10,000 marks should be collected. These powers dated back to April 1246, but Henry III and the English had resisted the execution of them as ' new and unheard-of extortion '.[3] But the Archbishop was that martial personage, Boniface of Savoy. He continued to act as captain of the Papal guards at Lyons, and the security of Lyons as a Papal asylum was absolutely dependent on the goodwill of the lords of Savoy, the three brothers Amadeus, Boniface, and Peter. It is difficult to say how much of the debts on the archbishopric were the legacy of preceding archbishops, and how much were the fruit of this Papal and Savoyard alliance. At any rate Innocent IV kept up a relentless pressure in favour of Boniface ; the registers of 1246–7–8 are full of imperative orders in the matter. Before the threat of excommunication both King and Bishops once more had to give way, the King earning the

Archbishop Boniface.

Complicity of Henry III.

[1] M. Paris, iv. 623.
[2] Register, Nos. 1935 to 3471, *passim* ; M. Paris, iv. 655.
[3] M. Paris, iv. 510.

'cordial maledictions of the whole country'[1]
because of his compliance. He had, in fact, his own
axe to grind at the Papal court. In the summer
of 1247 he had taken the vow of Crusade, and
himself allowed his motive to become transparent
by securing to himself a Papal grant of the sums
collected in England by pious gifts for the Holy
Land or by commutation of Crusaders' vows.[2]
Parliament had flatly refused him a grant in July
1248, and he was in such straits that he had to
sell his plate and jewels in London.[3] Yet his
attitude showed he had some strong secret hope ;
'the servant is not above his master. . . . I shall
appoint such ministers as I please,' was the answer
he had made to their demand for ministers, and
he consoled himself by the reflection that his
treasures would come back to him as rivers all
flow into the sea. They had been sold to 'those
boors the Londoners, who call themselves barons,
usque ad nauseam' ; whose wealth was a well of
riches,[4] and wells are made to be pumped. But
meantime his reliance was on the vow of Crusade
he had just taken, and which now was turned
into a bond negotiable at sight by a Papal concession issued August 1247, but not put into force
till immediately before this Parliament. This is
the secret of the bankrupt King's fit of self-assertion

---

[1] M. Paris, v. 36–8.

[2] Register, No. 4055 (August 1248).

[3] M. Paris, v. 22.   [4] Ibid. iv. 547.

and unusual superiority to Parliamentary grants.
Thus the way in which the Pope at this juncture The Pope's
handled the burning question of Provisions attitude
becomes intelligible. The number of cases was about Provi-
kept few, but the principle was maintained by the sions.
cases being very striking ones.   Since the remon-
strance received at Lyons in the close of the spring
of 1247, down to the end of 1248, the Registers
contain not much above a score of documents
which are acts of arbitrary interference with rights
of the English Church.   Out of 1,805 documents
included in that year and a half, twenty-eight
distasteful acts is not a large number, especially
as the total number which deal with English
affairs is so large, 142 out of the 1,805 ; of these
twenty-eight only ten are acts of Provisions for
foreigners in English benefices.   Marino, Papal
vice-chancellor, is to get preferments in Worcester
diocese up to 200 marks a year ; [1] a chaplain of
the Cardinal Bishop of Porto, is to be ' provided '
for by the Archdeacon of Sudbury ; [2] the Dean of
Wells, John Saracen, himself a Papal chaplain, is
to find the following warm berths,[3] for a scion of
the noble house of Vico, preferment of not less
than thirty marks, for a member of the Roman
civic family of Pappazini, not less than twenty
marks ; Guy de Foliano,[4] a Parma cousin of the
Pope, is to have a cathedral stall in Salisbury ;

[1] Nos. 3061, 3062.   [2] No. 3947.
[3] Nos. 3743, 3772.   [4] No. 3789.

six other documents [1] record that the Archbishop
of York and the Bishop of Salisbury, amongst
others, have purchased for themselves protection
against such Provisions. Other documents [2] empower the holding of pluralities by John the
Frenchman, Master Paganus a Papal clerk, one of
the Rossi of Parma, Matthew a Papal scribe, John
Odolino Papal subdeacon. Others [3] commission
Papal officials to secure to Richard of Cornwall the
share promised him long ago of the Crusading
moneys, or empower [4] Peter Saracen to raise £40
on the Bishop of Durham's bond, or authorize the
Bishop of Bath and Wells [5] to deprive of their
benefices all pluralists and sons of priests, unless
they can produce Papal dispensations.

One is a good illustration of the Pope's judicial
supremacy. Philip Ashley [6] had resented the Papal
'reservation' of the Church of Long Itchington
to the Roman noble who was Bishop of Bethlehem.
When the Bishop's proctor appeared, he was
beaten, had two ribs broken, his horse's tail was
cut off, and he and his horse tied up to one stall
together. When the Dean of Wells tried to put in
force his power as a Papal commissioner, Philip.
Ashley had persuaded the royal bailiffs to interpose
and to take security of 200 marks from the bishops'

---

[1] Nos. 2584, 2793, &c.
[2] Nos. 3002, 3425, 3987, 3988, 3991.
[3] No. 3528.   [4] No. 3580.   [5] No. 4009.
[6] Register, No. 3742.

proctors that they would not proceed. Philip is therefore cited to appear within two months before the tribunal of the Pope himself.

The Papal Registers therefore give ample proof that all the hot protestations of English clergy were as vain as spray upon the crags.

Further evidence is given by Matthew Paris. Cases in As an example of the miseries that came daily Matthew Paris. upon England he tells what befell the monks of Abingdon and the monks of Bury.[1] The best living in their gift, that of St. Helen's, Abingdon, worth 100 marks a year, was claimed the very day it fell vacant by a Roman ' provisor ' who had been biding his time. But the very same day the King demanded it for his half-brother Æthelmar of Provence, though Æthelmar already held so many benefices that he hardly knew their names. The abbot, douce man, finding himself between the upper and the nether millstones, decided for the King and against the foreigner who would be ' a thorn in his eye '. The Pope cited the abbot to Lyons. Old and ill as he was, he had to go ' in sorrow and fear and bitterness ', and eventually to console the Roman with a pension of fifty marks.

The monks of Bury St. Edmunds could not get their new abbot confirmed till they had bound themselves to pay 800 marks to a creditor of the Pope. One of the monks died at Lyons, one at Dover on his way back in bitterness of heart. The

[1] M. Paris, v. 39–40.

Y

blame for all this the chronicler lays upon the pusill-
animous conduct of our miserable king (*regulus*),
and he sums up the year 1248 as one of ' disaster to
the reputation of the court of Rome, that court
without courtesy or mercy, which is manifestly
threatened with the wrath of God '.[1]

Summary of results, 1245–50. The results of the years from the meeting of the
Council of Lyons, 1245, to the death of Frederick II,
1250, may be grouped under four headings : The
working of Provisions, the practical value of the
plenitudo potestatis, the parallel between France
and England and their differences, with the effect
of Henry III's weakness of character and his
peculiar circumstances, and finally the epoch-
making consequences of Innocent IV's pontificate.

Why Provisions were so hated. (1) Much that was healthy, and much that was
conscientious, went to make up the embittered
English feeling against foreigners in the early
thirteenth century. There was more in it than
mere insular prejudice, mere greed of office and
rivalry over court favour. It was by foreign
swordsmen that John had fought his way back
to despotic power and defiance of Magna Charta.
It was foreign nobles from his mother's land of
Poitou and foreign princes from his wife's kinsmen
of Savoy who incited Henry III to drive away his
constitutional ministers, and who took their place
and so aided his arbitrary rule. It was foreign
nominees thrust into English prelacies who were

[1] M. Paris, v. 47.

the obedient henchmen of the Papacy in the task of appropriating the preferments of the English Church, and draining her revenues. The people had but now attained to a real national unity. To resist new alien intrusions was a sound and natural instinct. The best men in the English Church were striving their hardest to raise her out of her insular lethargy, ignorance, and immorality. To them the wave of absenteeism and pluralism seemed to be likely to undo all their efforts. No wonder that the abuse of Provisions constituted the crucial point of discontent against the Papacy. They made the two chief grievances presented by the English envoys at Lyons, and the chief part of Innocent IV's promises. Inflexible as he was about taxing the clergy, even Innocent IV found it well to temporize about Provisions. In France he was plainly told that he was breaking his own laws, he was doing more than all previous Popes added together, he was ruining the French Church ; and all these three charges referred to the abuse of Provisions. What an abuse it was, in fact, the Papal Registers show on every page. Before the just wrath of King Louis the Pope gave way, and 1248–50 saw many fewer Provisions in France. In England, the reduction was from the spring of 1247 to the end of 1248. But there were before the end of that time at least several conspicuous cases.[1]

[1] A case not in the Register is that of a Papal Chaplain who

The *ple-* 　(2) The period is full of evidence how completely
nitudo
pote- 　accepted was the theory of *plenitudo potestatis.*
statis.　The limits attempted to be set to it by the canonists
of the twelfth and even of the early thirteenth
century have melted away. 　Even the most
passionate appeals stop midway to affirm their
loyalty to the principle. 　The Holy See is the
pillar set up by God, not man. 　There needs no
more than the mere whisper of an interdict, and
all active resistance dies down. 　Rebellion is as
the sin of witchcraft. 　That the Pope is above
human laws, that he is the judge of the whole
earth, that his power is unlimited, that he can act
as he chooses, these admissions come in the very
midst of King Louis's protests. 　If, then, the Pope
yields, it is not to mere talk, however big, but
for some incidental reasons of policy. 　For even in
Matthew Paris's documents the clergy avow their
moral indebtedness, and assert their unshakable
allegiance ' by every tie of love, obedience, and
devotion '. 　It was well realized at Lyons that
these expressions were sincere, that they out-
weighed irritation however strongly worded and
however justly felt, and that they could be safely
exploited still further. 　The cases of John of
Burgundy,[1] of the Papal nephews and Papal
hangers-on all provided for in 1247–8, the cases

is ' provided ' to the next prebendal stall at St. Paul's, and to
receive meantime an annuity of equal value from the Bishop
of London. P. R. O. Papal Bulls, xx. 44. 　　[1] No. 4045.

of the abbeys of Abingdon and Bury, are quite logical. These, and such as these, are the answers made to English supplications, because the supplicants had, at the very outset, given away their case.

(3) Many things combined to put England in a position far worse than that of France. Louis IX was a strong ruler, a heroic warrior, a shrewd man of affairs who need not appeal to his saintship. Henry, ' the king of simple life,' was one of those who bring religiousness into discredit. He had a difficult part to play as a vassal of Rome, and he made it more difficult by so often needing the aid of Rome to job a relative into some prelacy, to get absolution for himself from some oath imposed,[1] or to get a finger into the Church pie. Then, again, the Gallican Church had held more than one trial of strength with Rome, on great questions of theology, of canon law and of ecclesiastical organization; whereas England only boasted of its unbroken tradition of obedience ;[2] she was the milch-cow of the Papacy. Innocent had to look to France for moral support against Frederick, and for security in his stay at Lyons ; he could not afford to have against him, besides the Emperor, the foremost ruler of Christendom, *rex Christianissimus*. He had also to look to France for the final

Contrast between St. Louis and Henry III.

---

[1] Cf. Papal confirmation of Henry III's revocation of grants, Bliss Register, 10 Kal. Feb. 1249.

[2] Cf. Ottobono's letters in *Eng. Hist. Review*, 1890, p. 100.

repression of the Albigenses, and for the future control of Provence, perhaps even already for a future King of Sicily.

All these reasons make it plain enough why, in the Registers, not France but England figures as the happy hunting-ground of pluralist and provisor, nephew and chaplain. Matthew Paris is much incensed by Henry III's desertions of the cause, by his bargaining for a share in the spoil, by his using the vow of Crusade as a plea to be allowed to tax the clergy. But all this made little, if any, difference. A king of Henry's position and necessities, and, above all, of his character and convictions, could have done nothing to stay the hand of the Pope. He was reminded that it was no use his kicking against the pricks. The hopelessness of the situation lay not in the pusillanimity of a *regulus,* but in the futility of setting up a tribunal of God upon earth and then expecting that it could live without a revenue and administer the whole world without taxing it.

Inno- cent IV an epoch. (4) Innocent IV had, in fact, made it impossible to find a way out except by a breach in the theory itself of absolute obedience. It was inevitable that all this exasperation should leave a permanent bitterness. Men saw that an irreparable blow was being dealt to the old feelings of affectionate loyalty. King, bishops, and barons all disclaim any design of rebellion, but all agree in predicting it. The potent word, 'Appeal to a General Council,' has been uttered. The change in attitude and language since Innocent's accession is unmistakable. The old confidence, the old reverence can never be recaptured. Even in France a deep rift was caused, and there was consciousness that the seeds of great changes were being sown, *aliquid grande monstrum*, what the English writer puts bluntly as a threatened repudiation of Rome, a manifestation of the wrath of God against her.

So few writers on England do us what we feel to be adequate justice that there is a natural bias in favour of one who starts off with the plain and simple truth that English character and demeanour, English churches and cities and castles, English rivers, meadows, forests, and fields, are each and all superior to those of any other country.[1] Then Matthew Paris is so equipped at every point with healthy English prejudices ; against the Welsh and Scots, against the French and foreigners in general, against Jews, against Jacks-in-office, against innovators or reformers especially in religious methods, against either injustice or incompetence in rulers. He is such a keen partisan for his own order, such a sturdy denouncer of iniquity in high places, so broad and human in his interests, yet not too learned or too critical in the pedantic sense, and quite untroubled by philosophic doubt, by literary fastidiousness, by religious ecstasies or terrors. He is a vigorous writer, but no stylist ;

Character of Matthew Paris.

---

[1] Liebermann's preface in *Mon. G. Ss.* xxviii.

full of good sense, free from any subtlety ; no
wordy moralizer, and what is still better, no windy
philosophizer. He had none of the indifferentism
or aloofness of the cloister, but is alive with all the
political passions, the outspokenness, the blunt
judgements of a man who has seen the world.
Hypocrisy or over-religiousness would be almost
equally repugnant to English readers, but his
monastic robe is neither a cloak for ugly things,
nor on the other hand does it hide his individuality
or make him hush up good stories against the great.
He appeals to us as a hard hitter and a good hater.
He has all the English respect for a lord along
with the English exaggeration of liberty as an end
in itself.   Monk as he is, he objects to undue
spiritual meddling either by popes or by bishops.
He has little patience with what he does not
appreciate, and is not above burking what he finds
inconvenient, or defending abuses if only they are
old and vested.   The respectable appeals to him
more than does the heroic, and seemly living more
than high thinking.   In fact the loftier side of
mediaeval thought hardly appears at all in him ;
its idealism, its mysticism, its tenderness, its
grandiose aims, its architectonic concepts, must all
be sought elsewhere.   In his merits and defects
alike, in his broad humanity and his marked
limitations, he is the mirror of his age and country.
All that is on the surface he reflects so that it
stands out before us, but he is no magician to make

us see what lies beneath, for he does not see this himself. His books bear out the personal present-ment he has left us of himself, a big, healthy, fresh, vehement, but not unkindly man, shrewd without being profound; sensible, limited, prejudiced; full of life and its dramatic interests, its tragic and its comic elements, its crimes and its scandals, its strifes, and its prizes, all ending in the dust.

No wonder that he has dominated English history. For he is always animated, vivid, life-like. Everything comes from him in the concrete, under a picturesque form. Events are dramatized, the characters express themselves in appropriate speeches, often in pithy apophthegms. A great occasion always finds him ready to do justice to it, to give it full stage effect. He was indefatigable in using original documents, in repeating the accounts given by eyewitnesses. Many Papal bulls, imperial and royal letters are found in him and nowhere else. Of many important events, like the Council of Lyons, his is the only contem-porary description. Thus the modern historian is often faced by the demoralizing alternative, whether he will be critical, cautious, and dull; or will accept Matthew Paris and make a good story. Most embrace the latter, and among other consequences we have the greatest ruler of the Middle Ages, the Emperor Frederick II, dressed up to be a figure romantic indeed and mysterious, even appalling, but not historical, not even human;

He has come to domi-nate English history.

and in the end such is the nemesis on those who
will make up history into a stage play, the Frederick
of popular fancy, the heretic, infidel, blasphemer,
the half-Mussulman debauchee, becomes not more
but less interesting than the man as he actually
was.

His testi-
mony
needs
sifting.
Before one can use Matthew Paris for the
European history of the time, his evidence has
to be very carefully scrutinized, for it ranges in
value from first-hand, priceless testimony to the
most extravagant and worthless gossip. I cannot
help feeling that something of the same caution,
though in a less degree, applies to his utility for
English history. We must allow for his bias in
many directions, for his limitations of mind, for the
incompleteness and varying worth of his sources,
for the way in which he wrote things down as
they came to hand, for his perfectly maddening
confusedness as to dates. This by itself needs to
be set straight before he can be safely used. To
take only one instance, he actually repeats the
same events at distances of months or even years.
I can only do justice to his chronology by applying
a remark made on a poor musician, 'As for any
notion he has of time, he might have been born
and bred in eternity.' I do not forget what an
advance is marked by Dr. Luard's edition in the
Rolls Series, but no one can work over the ground
without desiring another and really critical edition
by some thorough scholar, in both the classical

and the historical senses of the word 'scholar'. Perhaps a syndicate of scholars would be needed.

Matthew Paris is first and foremost a monk ; next to that, he is an Englishman ; therefore he is also a political partisan. Fourthly, he has his omissions and defects. In robustness, in industry, As a mo-in eagerness, in strong language, he is a Macaulay nastic chroni-minus the style. He is also a Macaulay in preju- cler. dice, in wilful blindness, in truculence, in lack of spirituality. He is the last of the great monastic chroniclers, as he is the greatest ; the last great name, too, among the English Benedictines.

Thus when we make allowance in his chronicle A Bene-for the *idola claustri*, we must remember what dictine cloister was the atmosphere of a Benedictine cloister of in 1250. the middle of the thirteenth century. Enormous corporate wealth, St. Albans being the wealthiest of all ; administered by a body of no great number, at Christ Church, Canterbury, no more than seventy ; no high moral or spiritual aims, though no gross neglect of a *quantum sufficit* of moral and religious duties ; their educational work being done by newer agencies, their external interests concen-trated on their estates, which so often represented a perversion of Church endowment ; their internal interests concentrated upon a truceless warfare against any control or supervision from without ; it sounds like the description of an Oxford College in 1850, but is an average Benedictine abbey of 1250. Once he utters a sentimental regret for the

zeal and austerity of a bygone day; once he
welcomes a scheme of ' reform ' as a *hostia de caelo
demissa*, but the reforms were simply the rule of
Benedict as modified in other abbeys of the order
and by a few decretals directed to the subject ;[1]
but when it came to actual reform he was up in
arms at once, as against Bishop Grosseteste, who
found it necessary to depose [2] in one year the heads
of eleven monastic houses. He avenges them by
telling an incredible story about the bishop's
cruelty,[3] and he boasts that St. Albans and
St. Edmunds gave refuge to those so deposed.
But we find that Grosseteste was not the only
bishop who was *malleus religiosorum*. On two
other occasions he shows how far prejudice can
carry him, when he says of Grosseteste, whom he
has to hail as a saint notwithstanding, that his
insistence on monks giving their vicars a living
wage was ' more to spite the monks than to
benefit the vicars ',[4] and when he defends the
preposterous insolence of Christ Church monks in
excommunicating Grosseteste during the vacancy
of the archiepiscopal see.[5] But unfortunately for
his own case, he gives us his own idea of what
a visitation ought to be.[6] First, two friendly
priors send notice they are coming as Papal

---

[1] M. Paris, vi. 175–85.
[2] *Ann. Monastici*, Dunstable, iii. 143.
[3] M. Paris, v. 227.   [4] Ibid. 300.
[5] Ibid. iv. 248.   [6] Ibid. v. 258.

delegates, for St. Albans is one of the four or five exempt abbeys which only the Pope can visit. This gave them ten days' notice, which on their petition is extended to thirty days. This interval the abbot used to patch up a truce between himself and his monks on all disputed points. When the visitors arrived, it is not surprising to hear that they found the abbey swept and garnished, and nothing needing amendment. A body thus privileged were raised above the storms and struggles in which the Church outside was involved ; even the struggle to escape military service did not concern the abbot, who had reduced his quota to six knights' fees.

Thus, to the general Church aims of his time, Matthew Paris, when not actually hostile, as he is to the movement for strengthening the hands of bishops, is at least comparatively indifferent. The great movement which brought religion, and religion in its purest form of a radiant transfiguring inward light, to the serf, the outcast, the leper ; the movement which, to use the striking phrase of Machiavelli, saved Christianity by restoring it to its first principles—this awakens no sympathy in him, but only a complaint that the world is seething with such new-fangled orders which have gone further downhill in thirty years[1] than monks in four hundred years ; they now erect buildings of royal splendour, and become Papal tax-gatherers, death-

His attitude to the Friars.

[1] M. Paris, iv. 511.

bed extortioners, casuistical confessors, fishers not
of men but money. What he resents most is the
popular belief that salvation is hardly possible
outside the Friar's frock, and the ' shameless and
desperate ' conduct of Benedictine monks who
migrate to them.[1] It is not without some satisfaction that he tells of the scandal created by the
contest between the two orders,[2] as to which was
the more ascetic, whether Franciscan bare feet
counted for more than Dominican vegetarianism;
or of their loss of popularity in London for succour-
ing some Jews,[3] and in Paris for innovations in
the University.[4]

As cen-
sor of
the
Papacy.

II. When we come, then, to Matthew Paris to
study the relations of England to the Papacy, we
must not expect to find in him any full or generous
recognition of its activity. To Grosseteste it is
the sun of our earthly sphere, the source of light
and life. But Matthew Paris seems to think that
the ecclesiastical should be assimilated to the
physical climate of England, and should learn to
do without the sun while admitting his indispens-
ableness to feeble southern races. His view is,
perhaps, partly a survival of older anti-Papal
traditions, such as the bold protest of Alexander
the Mason (1212),[5] who came to such a bad end,
against Papal interposition in the secular affairs of
kingdoms ; or even the striking argument put

---

[1] M. Paris, iv. 280.   [2] Ibid. 279.   [3] Ibid. v. 546.
[4] Ibid. 529.   [5] Wendover, iii. 330.

forth by Bishop Gerard of York [1] at the dawn of the twelfth century, denying the primacy of Rome. But more probably it is to be explained as made up of three elements. The historic element is wrath at John's vassalage to Rome ; this comes out in his declaration that the ' detestable parchment ' [2] was burnt at Lyons in May 1245, which it was not. The second element is the dogged resistance to all Papal demands of money, which even leads him to the childish suggestion that the Pope might ' live of his own ', i.e. maintain a world-organization out of scanty and, what was worse, unpaid rentals of one nominally subject province in Italy. The third element which goes to form his view is simple illogicality. He cannot deny the *plenitudo potestatis*, yet will not have it exercised. He cannot deny that the Pope has power over the Church, but tries to ride off on a futile distinction between *dominium* and *cura*.[3] He admits the Pope is God's Vicar, yet compares the merit of opposing him *pro libertate ecclesiae* [4] to the merit of the martyr of Canterbury. He is driven at last to regard even a Crusade as inadequate justification for taxing the clergy, and to point to the fate of St. Louis as the penalty for such sacrileges.[5]

In the great duel between Papacy and Empire

---

[1] *Mon. Germaniae*, iii. 642 (*De lite sacerdotii et imperii*).
[2] M. Paris, iv. 417.   [3] Ibid. 39.
[4] Ibid. v. 525, 540, 653.   [5] Ibid. 171.

he is for a long time on the side of the Emperor,
whom he defends in a series of scathing comments
on the Papal manifesto of 1239 ; and he says the
manifesto failed because the whole world was
estranged from the Papacy by its avarice.[1]   He
scorns Henry II for publishing the excommunication against his own brother-in-law. With Innocent IV, however, he says all shame was laid aside.
Provisions which had hitherto spared lay patrons
now became daily. So the chronicler comes to
look to Frederick to free England from this Papal
tribute, and he makes St. Louis complain that in
refusing Frederick's advances in 1246, the Pope
had not acted as one who called himself *servus
servorum Dei* ; [2] and St. Louis's brothers threaten
(1250) that France will revolt if the Pope will not
make peace with the Emperor.[3] So far does his
partisanship go that he suggests that two Tartar
envoys to the Pope in 1248 were being persuaded
by secret interviews, presents of scarlet robes and
furs, and so on, to make a diversion by attacking
Frederick's ally, the Greek Emperor.[4] Think what
such a charge meant in 1248. Two and a half
centuries later, even a Borgia Pope found it more
seemly to perjure himself than to admit an
alliance with the Ottoman.

What, then, explains Matthew Paris's abandon-
ment of the Emperor after the Council of Lyons ?

[1] M. Paris, iv. 9, 100, 101, 547, 561.   [2] Ibid. 524.
[3] Ibid. v. 175.   [4] Ibid. 38.

Partly, the excommunication ; the dread words may have been unjust, *sed magna est vis eorum,* and, once they were spoken, the Emperor was in fact and law outcast from the Church. Partly, and perhaps mainly, the Emperor's rash letter to lay princes touched the monk of St. Albans in his tenderest part, the pocket ; for Frederick had 'hardened his heart and brought out his long-conceived venom, the old story, to reduce the clergy of all orders to their position in the primitive Church, to apostolic poverty '.[1]

He ventures to say that the Pope may be no true Pope but a heretic ; though it is safer to put such a word first into the mouth of a madman, who announces the Devil is loose ; [2] thirteen years later the Chronicler, getting bolder against Innocent IV, will put it into the mouth of a dying Bishop.[3] But at this time, 1245, it is the Emperor whom he charges with heresy for this attack on the Church. But even while brandishing the charge of heresy against the Emperor, he can spare a back-hander for the Papacy. ' If she succeeds now, the Church of Rome will assume to depose any prince or prelate, and low-born Romans will say, " We trampled down the mighty Frederick, who art thou to dream of resistance ? " ' [4]

Instead of being representative of his age on this question of submission to the Papacy, Matthew

His inconsistency.

---

[1] M. Paris, iv. 474–8.
[2] Ibid. 33.
[3] Ibid. v. 402.
[4] Ibid. iv. 478.

Paris represents an extreme position. He is like that millionaire who said, ' Merely to be *asked* for money makes me feel positively ill.' The one constant quantity in all his charges against the Papacy is extortion of money or money's worth. Historians have been somewhat too ready to assume that his attitude was the typical and normal one, whereas, when viewed in its proper environment and background, we can see it was (1) extreme, perhaps unique in its vehemence; (2) perfectly natural in a man of his views, (3) perfectly illogical. For even he admits that one or two precedents ('ne ad consuetudinem traheretur') admitted will rivet the Pope's claim for ever ; that is, one or two practical instances will deprive the Englishman of his favourite blundering refuge, the power of saying, ' The theory holds good of course, but in practice . . . ? ' That is, Matthew Paris really admits the theory, but hopes to raise objections to each proposed application of it.

Let us realize that when first he shows his fury at any Papal exactions, Matthew Paris stands almost alone as an extreme reactionary. Next let us realize that in fifteen years, 1239–54, or even in nine years, 1245–54, the national sentiment had caught up to him and reached the advanced position. We shall be able then, and only then, to measure and to appreciate the havoc wrought by Innocent IV.

But we must not part from Matthew Paris
ungratefully. He is the greatest historical writer
of the greatest mediaeval century. He is wonderfully good reading, if rather mixed good reading. In
the forlorn land of arid annalists and platitudinous
sermonizers he is a real man of flesh and blood.
We owe it to him that the thirteenth century is
alive to us ; we owe to him many of the best
stories in our history and some of our deepest and
dearest prejudices. Let us not be ungrateful.

LECTURE V

AIMS OF PAPAL POLICY, 1250–4. THE DUEL
OF PAPACY AND EMPIRE

FRA SALIMBENE OF PARMA, when challenged by his brother friar with being a believer in the prophecies of the Abbot Joachim, admitted that he had believed, 'but after the great Emperor died and then the year 1260 went by, I dropped all that doctrine, and mean to believe only what I actually see.' According to Joachim the Old Testament represented the age of God the Father, and His ministers were the patriarchs and prophets; the second age was that of God the Son, working by the Apostles and their successors; the third age was to be that of the Holy Ghost, and His ministers should be the monastic orders. This third age was to begin 1260, and was to witness the opening of the seventh seal of Revelations and the letting loose of Antichrist.

The thirteenth century was full of prophecies of this kind; a large part of the religious world implicitly followed Joachim; Merlin still circulated; there were no less than ten Sibyls in vogue; there were Eastern seers like 'the son of Agap who knew the courses of the stars'; even a cardinal in 1256 prophesied the speedy coming of a new

Emperor from out of the mountains and caves, who
should fill the whole earth with his roaring, but
then would rule like a lamb.

All this by a modern would be expressed, perhaps A turn-ing-point
not really better expressed, as a ' Zeitgeist ', a in Papal
consciousness that a decisive epoch in world-history history.
was at hand. Between 1240 and 1260 the Papacy
had passed the turning of the ways. Nowhere is
this better illustrated than in its dealings with
England. In tracing these I have already reached
the year 1250, and the King's vow of Crusade.

The Middle Ages were pretty well used to Mediae-val prin-
the practice of money *commutations*. Feudalism ciple of
assessed its duties ; the law, its list of crimes ; commu-tation
religion, her grades of sin,—all had their price.
You could buy off everything, from the bailiff's
order to go nutting for your lord, or the disability
to advance a villein's son to orders, up to the
offended majesty of the King, or the very wrath
of God Himself.

But even mediaeval matter-of-factness was
startled by the extension now given to the principle
in regard to Crusading vows. It was not merely that
the term 'Crusade' was extended from heretics to
schismatics, from schismatics to political enemies.
It had been a Crusade to burn Albi and Carcas-
sonne ; it was now declared a Crusade to attack
Greek Christians, even to take arms against the
Advocatus ecclesiae. With this extension the idea
lost much of its original potency. Worse still,

when it suffered commutation of form as well as diversion of aim, ' the Friars Preachers and the Friars Minor sent round their tax-collectors to extract by any argument from Crusaders their journey-money.'[1] They accepted vows from even the aged and the sick, and next day or on the spot released the vows for money down, and this money then all went straight into the coffers of Earl Richard of Cornwall in satisfaction of sums promised to him to help his Crusade, which was over and done with eight years before.[2]

applied to Henry III's vow of Crusade.

It was natural, therefore, that when Henry III took the Cross, March 6, 1250, many said it was only to extort money by the aid of the Papacy; and the Abbot of St. Edmunds taking it too was only *in derisum omnium*.[3] At Henry's request those Crusaders who were ready to start were ordered to wait for him. One-tenth of Church revenues for three years was to be collected and paid the King when ready to start. But this he did not even expect to do till the summer of 1256. Meantime, however, he got the ransoms from those who wished to commute their vows for money, and these came to a large sum. But his personal example could not prevail upon more than three of his courtiers to take the Cross. And the solemn and urgent preaching of two bishops and the Abbot of Westminster left the Londoners unmoved.

[1] M. Paris, iv. 9 ; vi. 134.   [2] Ibid. v. 73.
[3] Ibid. 101.

When he called the citizens 'ignoble money-grubbers' they muttered that his Crusade was only a plea for extortion. That the noblest motive force in mediaeval life had sunk to an object of suspicion and contempt was the natural result of the abuse of it in Papal hands for half a century past. *Hanc pertinaciam Roma parturivit* is not an unjust verdict, even if we must reject the bitter French reproach, that St. Louis's disaster was the fault of the Pope, who 'had for corrupt motives prevented Crusaders going out to Egypt, and sold them to Earl Richard and other nobles as the Jews sold doves in the temple '.[1]

The vow of Crusade was not the only sign of Henry's growing pliability to Romish influences in these years. As his debts multiplied and his difficulties increased, he looked more and more to the power that could open to him the purse of the clergy, allow him to repudiate his debts and revoke his grants, and assist him to fat preferments for his foreign relatives and their hangers-on. His relation to the Papacy came to be that caustically described by Matthew Paris : ' like a child that runs to its mother to complain whenever hurt or offended.' The Pope, on the other hand, had more and more need of the friendship of the English court. In 1250 he was chafing under the ' Savoyard fetters '.[2] Worse still, the Savoyard counts were beginning to think they had got all they could

His closer alliance with Rome from 1250.

---

[1] Ibid. 188.   [2] Ibid. 226.

squeeze out of the Holy Father, and to listen to
the golden offers of the Emperor. The Imperial
arms were gaining fast through 1250, and France
was urging him to peace. It seemed as if the
Pope must look out for another city of refuge. He
backed up Henry III in a dispute with Grosseteste,
who had excommunicated the Sheriff of Rutland ;[1]
and it was not common for the Head of the Church
to give away a single point in this matter to the
lay power. He held a long and secret conference at Lyons with Earl Richard of Cornwall, on
April 3, 1250. ' Thus the very day that the Sultan
took King Louis prisoner, the Pope was baiting
the hook to catch Earl Richard.'[2] The rumour
had it, that the object of the conference was to
induce the earl to undertake the decaying Latin
Empire of Constantinople. But another version
ascribed the Pope's action to an eager desire to
be allowed to take refuge in Bordeaux or even
in England itself, for men said from Bordeaux was
not a long voyage to England, and England would
only be the worse for the presence of the Papal
Curia—would be 'defiled' was the ugly word used ;[3]
the Papal agents and usurers were quite bad
enough. This was in December 1250, and it was
in December 1250 that the great Emperor died
suddenly, and the face of the world was changed.
The motive that, in what Henry was pleased to

[1] M. Paris, v. 109–10.   [2] Ibid. 159.
[3] Ibid. 189 ' coinquinari . . . maculari '.

call his mind, had balanced the fear of France and of Frederick, was the desire to get confirmed the appointment of Æthelmar or Aymer de Lusignan to the bishopric of Winchester.[1] He was no more than a boy, not yet fifteen years old; he was not in real orders, he was grossly illiterate; but he was Henry's half-brother of that favoured family of whom William was Earl of Pembroke; Guy was crusading at Henry's expense, and had already 500 marks a year from him and many other gifts; Geoffrey held the wardship of the barony of Hastings; the sister Alice was married by the King to the youthful Earl of Warrenne. Guy had some good qualities, but the other brothers were greedy, roistering swashbucklers; Geoffrey was charged before the Pope with boiling a servant alive, and preferred not to meet the charge.[2] Aymer already held more revenues than most bishops; the King had vainly tried to foist him on to the monks of Abingdon and the canons of Durham. Now he posted down to Winchester and harangued the monks from the cathedral pulpit. The monks were perhaps not more converted by the sermon than people usually are by sermons, but they had no choice save to yield, for they knew the Pope would annul any other election. ' Holy Father, why defilest thou Christendom by such deeds ? Justly art thou an outcast and a wanderer, . . . God of vengeance,

Aymer, Bishop of Winchester.

---

[1] Ibid. v. 183, 189.　　　　　[2] Ibid. vi. 406.

when wilt thou sharpen thy sword that it may drink the blood of such evil-doers ?' [1]

By 1253 the alliance in this matter of Church elections between Pope and King had gone so far that free elections had become a farcical term, and the whole bench of bishops presented to the King Henry's a protest. But they made the tactical error of sketch of presenting it by four of the very men whom the his own King had thus intruded, and Henry III, who said nomi- almost as many witty things as he did foolish nees. things, took the opening. ' I repent of the past and call on you four to help me make amends by handing in your resignations. For it was I who raised to the see of Canterbury you, Boniface ' (here a line has been discreetly erased in the MS.), ' It was I who raised from low estate you, William of York, my drawer of writs and paid judge, to be bishop of Salisbury; and you, Silvester, the lick-plate of my chancery, to be bishop of Carlisle. It was I who forced upon the monks of Winchester you, my brother Aymer, when in point of years and knowledge you should still have been under the usher's rod.' [2] The usher would have wanted all his appliances to make a decent pastor out of Aymer, who, five years later, was singled out, in May 1260, by the united baronage of England as the stone of offence to the whole kingdom, the enemy of righteousness and peace, the weaver of lies, the lover of darkness, the hunter of filthy

[1] M. Paris, v. 185.   [2] Ibid. 374.

lucre ; whose officers beat to death a clerk who had encroached on Aymer's rights of presentation ; who was himself popularly believed to have poisoned the Earl of Gloucester and other English nobles ; who was never even at school ; who was only in acolyte's orders ; who was not consecrated bishop till the last months of his life ; who, even apart from his see, had revenues greater than the Archbishop of Canterbury.[1] The appointment was regarded as a great concession wrung from Rome ; hence in a fit of anger, eighteen months later, Henry replied to his half-brother's episcopal fare-well, commending him to the Lord God, by saying, ' I commend you to the living devil. It was I who promoted you against the will of God and His Saints, and the will of the rightful electors.' [2] But Rome, in Matthew Paris's phrase, was not used to plough the sands ; the price she exacted was a provision of 500 marks a year for the Duke of Burgundy's son, Robert, a child.[3]

The final stage in the ill-starred alliance of the English and the Roman courts was the offer of the crown of Sicily, first to Henry's brother, then to his second son. Earl Richard had twice already been solicited to accept this *damnosa hereditas*. In 1247, says Matthew Paris, on the death of Henry of Thuringia, the Imperial crown was offered to the Count of Geldern, the Duke of Brabant, and

The offer of the Sicilian crown

---

[1] Ibid. vi. 401, &c.   [2] Ibid. v. 332–3.

[3] Ibid. 324.

then to Earl Richard 'quia vafer et abundans
nummis et quia frater regis Angliae'. This statement receives much indirect confirmation from
the Papal registers about this date.[1]

Again in 1250, as Richard came back from the
East, he was received at Lyons with extraordinary
honours by the Pope, and had long secret conferences with him. One rumour said that he was
offered the Eastern Empire ;[2] another that he
was sounded as to the Pope's coming to England.
But the later offer of 1252 is described by the
Papal biographer as a resumption of that made
already—that is, in 1250. Now in August 1252
a Papal letter to Henry III begged him to put
pressure on his brother, to whom also Papal bulls
were sent direct, followed in November by the
Papal notary, Albert of Parma.[3] Then, as now, an
English lord fulfilled the conditions in Italian eyes,
refused of being at once rich and stupid. But Richard
by
Richard, was quite clever enough to see why he was to
be made a cat's-paw. He pleaded ill health, inex-
perience in war, and unwillingness to supplant a
nephew, Henry, Frederick's son by Isabella. When
further pressed, he demanded guarantees in money
and fortresses and hostages. Finally he told the
nuncio it was a case of 'I give you the moon, go

[1] M. Paris, iv. 561 ' occultas causas ' ; cf. v. iii, 118 :
Regesta, 4617, 7752, 7902–3, 7905–6, 7911.

[2] Ibid. v. iii, 118, 347.

[3] Rymer, i. 284, 288 ; Berger Register, ii. cclxxix ; Muratori,
Antiquitates, vi. col. 104.

up and take it '.[1] From Richard of Cornwall the
Pope turned again to Charles of Anjou, but Charles
refused, June 1253.[2] So the Pope turned back once
more to England. His nuncio had seen that the
King was not proof against the lure. To Henry, an
impenitent prodigal and an irreclaimable bankrupt,
all gold was glittering, even the fairy gold of the
Sicilian crown. He jumped at the offer of it for
his second son Edmund, February 1254.[3] Conrad's
death (May 1254) made no difference, for Innocent
needed Edmund as a second string to his bow even
while he was thinking of taking up Conradin.[4] The
Pope urged Henry to take action ; he transmuted
his crusading vow into one for Sicily, he extended
his leave to tax the clergy from three years to
five, he pledged himself to pay the King £100,000
as soon as Henry started, a Greek calends date.
Meantime, however, the pecuniary tide was to set
the other way. Henry was made to stand surety
for the immediate debts of the Holy See, and next
year to undertake the reimbursement of all expenses hitherto incurred, which were reckoned at
134,541 marks.[5]

accepted by Henry III for Edmund.

This was the sum charged by the next Pope,
Alexander IV, to confirm the arrangement, and he
also made the King renounce the claim to the
£100,000. Henry was thus fast limed ; and the

Results for Eng-land.

---

[1] M. Paris, v. 457, 680.
[2] *Register*, Nos. 6811, 6819.   [3] M. Paris, v. 361, 458.
[4] Rymer, i. 202–3 ; Berger Register, ii. cclxxxv.
[5] Rymer, i. 337.

four years 1255–8 inclusive are taken up with his
struggles [1] to scrape up all and any sums of ready
money to send to Rome, his borrowings, mort-
gagings, plunderings, his desperate shifts and straits
as a sort of royal Micawber before the remorseless
and insatiable dunning of a creditor, who began by
telling him that he must cut down for this greater
object all his expenditure on works of piety ; who
sent him blank forms ready sealed for issue to the
abbeys, charging them with sums of 400 and 600
marks, and taking all the wool crop of the Cistercians; who mortgaged the King's credit right and
left to Italian moneylenders, and dispatched them
to England with assurance of instant payment;
who threatened his helpless debtor with excommunication when the nation turned mutinous; who
made him buy dearly each adjournment; who made
him levy taxes on the clergy and impounded
the proceeds midway ; who had three successive
agents in England to see that the screw was kept
on ; and who finally, when the country had been
driven to revolution, revoked the original grant
and declared all the instalments forfeit.[2]   Every
motive was exploited that could be found in
a character like Henry's : personal ostentation,
family pride and affection, religious scrupulosity;
he was plied with flattery, bribes, reproaches,
menaces, and ecclesiastical censures, all in turn.
In 1254 soldiers were engaged on letters of credit

[1] Rymer i. 316, &c.   [2] Ibid. 428.

drawn in his name. In 1255 £4,000 was accepted on account, and he was told he must send money and troops immediately. In January 1256 he was asked if he was going to let the mortgagees foreclose on the very churches of Rome ; in May he was pledged to find 60,000 marks for Siennese creditors of the Papacy, and 10,000 for the Pope and Cardinals ; in June there were three sets of bankers, each guaranteed to receive prior payment to any others ;[1] in September, so desperate was the situation, that an attempt—a vain attempt— was made to wring a contribution from Scottish purses.[2] In 1257 the Pope talked of issuing an interdict ; and actually proposed a tax of one-third of the whole realm of England. It was said that Henry's debt now amounted to 350,000 marks.[3] Men said Pope and King were now bound in an alliance of shepherd and wolf against the sheep. The clergy, helpless against their joint oppressors, caught between hammer and anvil, agreed to pay 42,000 marks, but insisted on confirmation of a list of thirty canons, for which they were ready to die like St. Thomas of Canterbury. Even Henry's incurable belief in something turning up now gave way. In offering to resign the Sicilian crown, he said three true things ; that he had paid a large part of the Church's expenses ; that the resistance of his prelates made it impossible for him to do more ; that he had taken up the cause from his

[1] Ibid. 343.   [2] Ibid. 349.   [3] M. Paris, v. 521.

devotion to the Church of Rome, rather than for temporal gain.[1] It was an unkind cut when the last Papal agent, Herlot, in his final report, attributed the whole failure to Henry's arbitrary modes of procedure and the unpopularity of the

National revolt in 1258.

foreign favourites.[2] These two causes had indeed made smouldering discontent for over thirty years; but what fanned it into the flame of 1258 was the fatal Sicilian affair.

These dealings as seen from the Papal side.

These dealings with England must now be studied from the inner or Papal side. England had been goaded into revolution by the business of the Sicilian crown. Her highest ideal, the tribunal of God upon earth, had been debased into a byword and a shame. And all for what ? To carry out a futile and suicidal project, the incorporation of

The goal of Papal policy

the Sicilian kingdom into the Papal states. This was the most pernicious consequence of the whole fateful legacy of policy left by Innocent III, to gather temporal sway into spiritual hands, to unite Popedom and kingdom. That masterful genius had had to bow even his inflexible will, to confess to failure after ten years of bitter disappointments. But the project he abandoned has proved an irresistible lure to Papal ambition ever since. It was the one infatuation that beset the clear hard mind of Innocent IV, that turned to ashes all the success which he had achieved by such superhuman strength of purpose and such outrage to morals

[1] Rymer, i. 359.   [2] *Ann. Monastici*, i. 464.

and to religion in his methods, and that at last, as men thought, broke his heart. As early as the Council of Lyons he had made up his mind, not merely to depose Frederick, but to disinherit Conrad too. The race of the Babylonian king was to be blotted out, the whole brood of the viper to be crushed.[1] Thrice did Frederick offer, and thrice in vain, to abdicate in favour of his son.[2] For some time a decorous show was kept up of not including Conrad in the irrevocable condemnation. The contemporaries [3] do not regard Conrad as expressly excommunicated or as beyond reconciliation. The Holy Father must not seem deaf to all offers of peace and penance, at least from the son. Nor could he afford to drive the neutral princes of Germany into Conrad's camp. Nor did it yet seem feasible to shake Frederick's position in Sicily without the aid of some foreign prince. The great plot to murder the Emperor in 1247 had only served to prove his strength, his promptitude, and his ruthless vengeance. Louis of France, too, had to be taken into account, who had in 1247 put great pressure on the Pope to accept Frederick's overtures.[4] But as soon as the sails of Louis were out of sight on their way to the East, Innocent declared, August 1248, that he

fixes the aim of Innocent IV from 1245,

led him to attempt conquest of Sicily 1248–9.

[1] Rodenberg, *Innocent IV u. Sicilien* ; Rodenberg, *Epist. Pontif.* 585, and 681, xvii.

[2] *Regesta Imperii,* 3511 ; M. Paris, iv. 523, v. 99.

[3] Nicolas de Curbio, p. 388 ; M. Paris, v. 248.

[4] M. Paris, iv. 523.

would never make terms with Conrad ; he issued
an extraordinary document to win over the
Sicilian clergy ; [1] he threw aside all the cardinals
who had been at his right hand since his election ;
he appointed the one man in whom he had come
to have sole confidence, and gave him extraordinary
powers, both temporal and spiritual, for the
invasion and conquest of Sicily ; everything was
arranged for the direct government of the land
by the Holy See itself, and Cardinal Peter Capocci [2]
was expected to carry this out as successfully as,
after a stay of eighteen months in Germany, he had
carried out the election of the second Anti-Emperor,
William of Holland, November 4, 1248. But
mundane warfare needs other qualifications than
does that of the Church militant. Things seemed
at first in his favour since Frederick's startling
recovery of all Piedmont and the Savoyard counts
in the last quarter of 1248. For these gains in the
West were balanced by the capture of Enzio, in
May 1249, and consequent defections in Lombardy
and Romagna. The Legate, during the winter of
1249–50, was able to win over nearly all the march
of Ancona. But with this he came to a standstill.
There was bad news from Germany,[3] which meant
a check in the supplies of pay from Lyons. The
Count of Manipello, with the first blast of his

---

[1] Dec. 1248, *Regesta*, 8056 ; Rodenberg, *Innocent IV und
Sicilien*, p. 65.   [2] Ibid. p. 70 ; *Epist. Pontif.* ii. 681, viii.
   [3] *Regesta Imperii*, 4987ᵃ.

trumpets, seemed to scare back to the Imperialist standard the fickle towns of the Mark. Above all, Frederick himself had recovered from the illness which had kept him inactive all the winter.[1] The old belief in their wonderful Emperor's invincibility was never stronger than with this blaze of success all along the line in 1250.[2] On the Rhine, too, Conrad was victorious. Now we see why the Pope took advantage of Earl Richard of Cornwall's return from the East to give him a most flattering reception at Lyons, to entertain him at dinner with unusual cordiality, and to have long and secret conferences with him. Now we see why, when the French princes pressed him hard to have peace, he began to take steps to get a refuge in Bordeaux.[3] For though the whole world believed the Pope beaten at last, yet he would not give in. He had to recall the Cardinal Peter, who was to have done such great things. He gave up the idea of a conquest of Sicily by a Church army under Church generals, and for Church advantage. He promised a new army and new captain for 1251. Then, on December 13, 1250, after only a few days' illness, the great Emperor died. Had he lived a year longer he must have won as he had won before.[4] He had overcome three Popes, and he must have

Frederick's victories in 1250.

Importance of his sudden death.

---

[1] *Regesta Imperii*, 3816.   [2] Ibid. 3823.

[3] Ibid. 3817ª.

[4] Cf. the Papal biographer, M. Paris, Salimbene, the Paduan chronicler, &c.

overcome a fourth. But it was a duel between
a man and an institution. The Papacy was an
organized system almost independent of the
personality of its rulers, greater certainly than
any one Pope. But the Empire was only a survival,
galvanized into occasional activity at considerable
intervals by some of the masterful inheritors of
the purple. All depended on the character, the
resources, and, most of all, the prestige of an
individual. Frederick had never stood so high
in reputation, so near to final triumph, as at that
moment.[1] ' He whom none could overcome,
succumbed to Death.' To Papal circles it was the
outstretched hand of God : ' He saw Peter's bark
near to shipwreck ; He struck down the tyrant
and saved her.'[2] On January 19, 1251, Innocent
had not yet heard the momentous news ; by the
25th[3] he had already written to Sicily to assure
to the cities free election of their magistrates, to
promise the barons new fiefs ; he had promised to
bring them his own presence ; he had reappointed
Cardinal Peter Capocci. The idea of a direct Papal
State had been revived in its fullness. The Cardinal
was allowed to bring over reluctant cities by
guaranteeing that they should be under no king or
lord, but in the demesne of the Church. Fanned
thus into flame, the old elements of disorder,
feudal, municipal, and racial, broke out all over

*The Pope
at once
revives
his
scheme,*

---

[1] *Regesta Imperii*, 3823.   [2] Nicolas de Curbio.
[3] *Regesta Imperii*, 3835[a].

the double kingdom. It is true that the iron frame of administration erected by the hand of Frederick withstood even these blows, and by the end of April 1251 Manfred had put down the revolt everywhere but in Campania. Yet Manfred himself came forward to offer submission to the Papacy, and with him came his kinsman and friend, the Marquis Berthold of Hohenburg, captain of Frederick's German troops. Innocent might at one stroke, without bloodshed or expense, have resettled the Holy See in its overlordship of Naples and Sicily, severed the dreaded link with Germany, divided the Stauffen House against itself, and reduced Conrad to harmlessness. All this he could have done but for the infatuated passion for direct Papal rule. Other motives concurred. His triumphal progress through Lombardy [1] had for the moment excited even his cool brain. His past successes beyond hope made him impervious to disappointment ; sooner or later Sicily must be his, anyhow. And was not Manfred after all one of ' the dragon's brood ' ? And was there not strife already sown between him and his legitimate brother Conrad ? So he only offered to Manfred but terms lower even than what he got under Frederick's failed again will.[2] Manfred refused, and the chance was gone. 1251. Innocent had again staked on the highest throw, and again was to lose the substance in grasping

[1] Nicolas de Curbio.
[2] Rodenberg, *Epist. Pontif.* iii. 100.

at the shadow. Once more his cardinal-general failed, and had to be recalled. Once more Papal resources were exhausted. In a few months the enemy might be again in the Patrimony of the See. It was a necessity once more to fall back on foreign intervention. But at this very juncture, January 1252, Conrad had arrived in Apulia and taken possession of his kingdom. Now Conrad had the illusion that the Church's great quarrel had been a personal one with his father. He knew that peace would be welcome to his own partisans in Italy, and to an important party in the Curia itself,[1] a party which now came forward, as it had done in 1245 and in 1247, and as it did in 1254 in the election of Alexander IV to be Innocent's successor. Nothing brings out in a stronger light the unshakable self-reliance of Innocent IV. He let the peace party try their hand because he was sure they would fail. He had the fortitude to shelve his own views for theirs during six months, and to give them complete and ungrudging support in order that their failure might be the more complete and signal. He withdrew Cardinal Capocci and appointed as legate the Cardinal Bishop of Albano, the leading exponent in the Curia of a conciliatory policy. To satisfy their desire for a more spiritual and less political line of action, he revived, by a series of measures from April to June 1252, the attack on heresy in the

then lets the peace party try with Conrad.

---

[1] Rodenberg, *Innocent IV u. Sicilien*, p. 117.

Lombard cities.[1] He restored to the churches in Germany, in Italy, and in Sicily their rights of free election of prelates, rights which he had snatched from them during the last four years, and in so doing he laid down what had been his chief weapon in the great struggle against the Empire. But his biographer, who had been his chaplain and confessor through his whole pontificate, betrays his master when he tries to defend him.[2] He argues that it was evident at once that the negotiations were a fraud on Conrad's part, because Conrad insisted on the Empire and Sicily as his rights, though he must have known these claims inadmissible. It was really Innocent who foresaw that Conrad would insist on these, and who was as far-sighted as Conrad was blind. How could the Papacy desert William of Holland in Germany or the Sicilians now enduring exile for their adherence to the cause of Rome ? How could the Papacy abandon that severance of Sicily from Germany which had been its watchword for sixty years ? That the negotiations continued to June 1252 is evidence of Conrad's honest but unstatesmanlike optimism ; it is evidence also of Innocent's shrewdness and self-restraint. After all On he gained time, and he gained the right to revert failure of the peace

---

[1] M. Paris, vi. 302. Conrad, in his manifesto of 1254, says he found heresy openly preached when he came to Milan, Brescia, and Mantua ; ' quia salva reverentia domini Papae, dicuntur ecclesiae filii speciales.' [2] c. 31.

party In-
nocent
resumes
his own
policy,

and of-
fers
Sicily to
Richard
and to
Charles.

to his own policy of no surrender. The point of departure is given by the withdrawal of legatine authority (June 17)[1] from the Bishop of Albano and the substitution of two vehement Sicilian prelates. But the change was not so soon known outside. As late as August 13[1] the Venetians were stipulating to be included in the peace expected, and the Pope gave the promise. But already, on August 3,[2] the offer of Sicily to Earl Richard of Cornwall was drawn up. Indeed, to save time, an identical form was prepared to be used on Charles of Anjou if Richard of Cornwall declined. Each was told that he had been unanimously chosen by the cardinals, and on each identical personal compliments were lavished. But the Papal envoy did not arrive in England till November 11, 1252 ;[2] and after that it took no less than eight months to be off with the first choice and on with the new. In this interval the Papal prospects had got steadily worse. Conrad was master of the whole kingdom except Naples, which he was besieging. His half-brother, Frederick of Antioch, was on the Abruzzi frontier, so that the Patrimony was threatened on two sides, while Brancaleone, as Senator of Rome, reduced Papal sovereignty to a nonentity. Against these results Innocent was powerless. He did not even send help to Naples. All he could do was to deal out promises of future

---

[1] *Epist. Pontif.* iii, under the dates given.
[2] M. Paris, v. 346–8, 368.

liberties to the Sicilian Church. He had still the
firmness to refuse Earl Richard's demands of
guarantees.[1] But as soon as he saw Richard was
not to be had on the terms, he lost not a moment [2]
in turning to Charles. The Papal biographer, to
ease the awkwardness of this transition, represents
that Charles, hearing of the offers made to Richard,
volunteered himself. The amount of truth contained in this statement is that Charles's first
impulse was eager acceptance, and that the dealings with Charles were well advanced even before
the final refusal had been received from Richard.
By mid-June 1253 Innocent was treating Charles's
acceptance as an accomplished fact. He sent full
powers to his envoy, Albert, to enable him to set
things in action at once, and empowered him
especially to borrow money, no matter from whom
or at what rate of interest, and to pledge all the
churches and abbeys in his Legation. He dispatched the deed of investiture sealed by all the
cardinals. He notified to his partisans in Sicily
the coming of the deliverer. Unfortunately, the
deliverer meanwhile had thought better of it. The
terms [3] had been not hard, except those stipulating
on behalf of the Sicilian clergy for complete freedom from lay taxation and jurisdiction, and from
any interference in their elections. When they

[1] Ibid. 457.

[2] 25 April Albert left England and by 12 June he had seen
Charles, got his acceptance, informed the Pope, and received
his ratification.   [3] *Epist. Pontif.* iii. 178–81.

seemed to stick in Charles's throat, the Pope threw
in the title of King, and went so far as to offer that
the terms should be submitted to the arbitration
of two prelates and a knight, to be nominated by
Charles himself ; but he added the remarkable
proviso that this was only a blind, and Charles
was to bind himself by letters-patent to make no
use of the further concessions thus obtained. This
was an ingenious response to Charles's plea that

Charles
draws
back at
the last.

his counsellors were against the project. The best
counsellor, however, was probably Charles's own
perception of the inadequacy of the resources of
Provence as against Richard of Cornwall, a prince
who was said to be able to put down a gold coin
for every silver one of the most wealthy man in
England. Perhaps also the offer of Hainault by
Margaret of Flanders to buy Charles's alliance
against the enemy, William of Holland, was already
in the air, though the offer was not actually made
till after July 4, 1253. In October Charles had
gone off to this new field of warfare ; Conrad
had taken Naples and was writing to his faithful
burgesses of Speier and Cremona that he was only
staying to collect treasure for a return to Lombardy
and Germany. The Romans had forced the Pope
to return to his city after nine years' absence ;[1] and

Revival
of the
peace
party.

this meant that he was once more entering into
the negotiations proposed by Conrad and deferring
to the peace party in the Curia. To convince

---

[1] M. Paris, v. 417.

them that he had sincerely entered into this path, he issued a document [1] which is a judgement out of his own mouth upon his whole pontificate. It admits that the practice of Provisions is hostile to *honestas* and to *ordo*, that it was forced on him by the iniquity of the times and the shamelessness of the office-seekers, and that it would be a mighty and triumphant joy to shake it off. He solemnly promises that henceforth only natives shall be appointed to church preferments in each country ; he declares that he does this at no one's solicitation, but of his own motion ; and ends with the extraordinary clause, 'Any one who contravenes this is exposed to God's curse and to ours ; any letters of ours that run counter to this may be torn up.' Such intrusion of a personal element is unprecedented in the briefs of Innocent IV. It shows what strong measures he was prepared to take that he might convince the peace party that the perversion of spiritual functions into political means had been forced on him by political needs. It shows also that he had to put down a very heavy concession by way of deposit to get the peace negotiations on foot again after past experiences. Indeed his objects were the same as during the former negotiations of the spring of 1252 ; first, to gain time ; second, to make the peace proposers learn for themselves that they were driving against a wall. A sort of compromise was

[1] *Epist. Pontif.* iii. 200.

The double dealing with Conrad and with England. arrived at by which through all the negotiations with Conrad a secret offer of the crown to the English court was being made. Many of the documents remain, though many more are now lost; but it is clear that the English court, which was in Gascony from mid-August 1253 to the end of 1254, was in constant and confidential correspondence [1] with Rome during the last six months of 1253, ostensibly about Henry's vow of Crusade, but assuredly also about Sicily, and with a curious degree of intimacy and mutual understanding.[2] It seems certain that the offer of the crown to Edmund had been made long before the conditions were accepted in December 1253, and the public announcement made in March 1254.

It would take months before any fruit could come of this new arrangement. Innocent's cue, therefore, was to spin out the time. Already Conrad had retired from the frontier to winter in Apulia. The formulation of the charges the Church had against him and the allowance of a space for his reply brought matters to March 22, 1254, and by this date the agreement with Edmund was safely ratified and sealed.

The part played by Thomas of Savoy. The man who perhaps did most to bring Henry III into the Papal nets was Thomas of Savoy, the most cosmopolitan [3] and versatile member of that shrewd and successful family,

---

[1] Papal Registers.   [2] Potthast, 15181.
[3] Rymer, i. 297.

true mountaineers and borderers like our own chieftains of the Scottish march, ' who sought the beeves that made their broth, In Scotland and in England both.' After an adventurous career in Flanders, he had returned to his native land to be bought over by fiefs from Frederick II, which he then secured by promptly ratting to the other side and marrying the Pope's niece. He professed the part of a peacemaker in Conrad's behalf, but was really acting in Papal interests. As the Queen's uncle, he was welcomed at King Henry's court in Gascony, where we find him with his two brothers in the spring of 1253. There, too, was Cardinal Ottobono, the Pope's nephew ; Peter Cacheporc, Archdeacon of Wells, and Peter Acquablanca, Bishop of Hereford. The one Englishman who by the side of these foreigners attests Henry's acceptance is John Mansel, the King's trusted clerk.[1] It does not appear that any of the difficulties which had deterred Charles presented themselves to Henry's sanguine mind, and he was got on much cheaper terms. He accepted also the fullest precautions for complete freedom of the Sicilian Church, as they were inserted by the Pope in his final revision of the agreement.

Sicily accepted for Edmund.

Conrad could not perhaps regard it as treachery that the Papal campaign should all these months be going on against him in Germany by appointment of a new legate, by preaching a Crusade, and

[1] *Epist. Pontif.* iii. 407.

by inviting William of Holland to come for coronation as Emperor. But this affair with England would be taken very differently by the young king, who had already been fooled in the same way twenty months before. Innocent betrayed what he feared by leaving Rome in April 1254 for the safe inaccessibility of Assisi, by being in a hurry to confirm the English treaty (May 14) and to act on it at once by allowing the Crusading tenth to be handed over, and by instructing Henry to crown the boy king and

But Innocent was only saved by Conrad's death.

provide him with a royal seal.[1] He might well be anxious. A boy of nine years old, even in an Apulian dress and with the symbols of royalty, backed by the I O U's of the most insolent sovereign in Christendom, did not constitute a very solid defence against a son of Frederick II, who had a victorious army, a united people, a full treasury, and a just case. A bitter, a not undeserved, and an inevitable humiliation apparently awaited the Pope, after all his shifts and turnings.

Was Henry III to save him? Would not a majority of the Pope's own counsellors welcome the downfall of what they deemed an unspiritual policy?

But not once or twice alone in history has death proved to be the Papacy's best ally. The institution is immortal; it has only to wait till the tyranny be overpast. If the tyrant dies

[1] Rymer, i. 302.

defeated, the lesson is obvious. If, as to Conrad's father and grandfather, to Frederick II and to Henry VI, death comes in the full wind of success, at the very moment of victory alighting on their ensigns, then still more is the Divine warning one that all may read. What, then, when the victor is in early manhood, when he is the third victim of his doomed family, leaving only an infant son! What could this be but a judgement of God in very deed, and could the Papal chancery do less than claim it for such? If anything was wanted to complete the dramatic total reversal of positions in May 1254, it was supplied by Conrad's own will and testament.

The words 'Church and State' represent what ought to be an alliance, but is in modern times at best a dualism and often an open warfare. Partly, no doubt, this is due to historical causes, the modern State taking its revenge for the long domination of the ecclesiastical power in the past, just as the maxim ' cuius regio eius religio ' marked a sixteenth- and seventeenth-century reaction of nations against the autocracy of Rome. But in large part the opposition of Church and State expresses an opposition between the two sides of human nature which we must not too easily label as good and evil, the heavenly and the earthly, the sacred and the profane. For the State, too, is divine as well as the Church, and may have its own ideals and sacramental duties and its own *Reflections on the duel of Papacy and Empire.*

Church and State have the same end.

prophets, even its own martyrs. The opposition of Church and State is to be regarded rather as the pursuit of one great aim, pursued by contrasted means. The ultimate aim of all true human activity must be, in the noble words of Francis Bacon, ' the glory of God, and the relief of man's estate.' And this aim may be approached either by the way of compulsion, organization, legislation, in fact by political means ; or else by the way of conviction and inspiration, in fact by the means of religion. If this be a just distinction, then where the Middle Ages failed was in attempting to unite the two spheres too closely, to make politics the handmaid of religion, to give the Church the organization and form of a political State, that is to turn religion from an indwelling spirit into an ecclesiastical machinery.

The mediae- val pas- sion to realize ideals.

This was an instance of that mediaeval passion for realization of its ideals, for their expression in concrete form and in practical conduct, which meets the student of the Middle Ages at every turn, and which makes it so hard to do justice to both aspects of the time. Thus the adoration for the land ' over whose acres walked those blessed feet, That bore for us the Cross on Calvary;' took shape as a fully equipped feudal kingdom of Jerusalem. The submission to texts such as ' Keep yourselves unspotted from the world ', and ' Take no thought for the morrow ', was materialized into the stone walls and the sackcloth of a cloister. The daily miracle of the universe was translated into wonder-working images and a swarm of angels and demons. Sin and despair, the moral struggle with its relapses and its victories, were transferred to a topo-graphical hell and purgatory. The bliss of the redeemed was located in the successive planetary spheres.

It was a beautiful and a generous impatience which thus sought to realize the ideal by giving it concrete form and local habitation. But in the nature of things it was foredoomed to failure ; the ideal thus brought down to earth takes on something earthy, it is subdued to the element it works in ; ' the Most High dwelleth not in temples made with hands.' Now the mediaeval Empire was an attempt to embody in actual work-a-day institu-tions certain ideas which were both true and deep, but not able to stand the strain of being thus materialized. Such were the ideas of a common European civilization based on a common official language, a faith held in common, and common principles in law, government, and society ; the idea of a common inheritance from ancient Rome ; and the idea of a common interest against the menacing outer worlds of heathendom and Islam. The mistakes were the endeavours to build out of these an actual political structure which should take in all Europe under one government, and to apply the name Roman Empire to this dream-fabric. But even this was not so profound a

The ideas which underlay the Empire.

mistake as the other, the Papacy's mistake of endeavouring to build religion into a state organization, to make the heavenly city into an earthly city, to set up a rival spiritual Empire. Have we not been warned, ' My kingdom is not of this world ' ? Worst of all when by a fatal logic it was argued that the head of this spiritual Empire must also be a temporal ruler, first of the actual city of the Seven Hills, then of the Latin and Sabine dominions adjoining the Patrimony of St. Peter ; then of the provinces of Spoleto, Ancona, Romagna, even Tuscany ; and finally of all south Italy and Sicily too. If the Emperor who called himself King of Kings and Caesar Augustus was the most unreal of mediaeval unrealities, the Pope who would be at once successor of the Apostles and feudal lord from the Rubicon to the sands of Africa was worse, he was a contradiction in terms. The Papal States were a veritable body of death to the true spiritual life of the greatest institution in human history. The mighty duel between these two great antagonists was not actually decided till

the day that Frederick II died. Could any one have saved the Empire from its inevitable doom, it was he with his genius for rule down to the minutest details, his marvellous fiscal organization, his clear-cut, patient, inflexible policy. 'Si Pergama dextra Defendi possent, etiam hac defensa fuissent.' Great man as he was, *stupor mundi*, the world's wonder, he could not avert the inevitable hour

but only delay it. His Roman Empire was not
an Empire ; for the union of western Christendom,
a very real union in some ways, was not and could
not be a political union. Nor was his power Roman,
real as it was, but a fortuitous concurrence of four
widely different elements : the kingdom of the
Sicilies where he was absolute, Germany where he
only existed by sufferance and at the cost of ever-
increasing bribes to the Princes, middle Italy
where he was accepted from fear of his arms and
as an alternative to Papal suzerainty, Lombardy
where he was only the head of one of the two
party leagues and that one the weaker of the two.

But among all these difficulties he with his genius,
his resources, and, above all, his infinite patience,
might have established a *modus vivendi* for
himself and one or two successors. What ruined
his Empire was that it came into collision with
the rival schemes of the Papacy, not merely the
Papacy as a spiritual power, though this alone
must have proved fatal to the Empire sooner or
later, for Christendom cannot serve two masters,
and if one must be chosen it will be the one who
claims to speak in the name of Christ. But what
precipitated this ruin was that he came into
collision with the Pope, not as Pope merely but
as Bishop of Rome, and suzerain of the old Latin
territory, claiming to be heir of the great Countess
Matilda, and secretly resolved to be direct ruler
of the kingdom of Naples and Sicily. It was the

Above all, the collision over the Papal States. fatal lure of a Papal State of the Church that determined the first excommunication of Frederick by Gregory IX, the invasion of his kingdom in his absence on Crusade by a Crusading host under the banner of the Cross Keys, the support treacherously given to his rebel subjects of the Lombard League, the second excommunication of him as a beast of blasphemy on a monstrous charge (the Three Impostors' story) which they had afterwards the decency to drop. And now it was the project of incorporating south Italy with those Papal States which made Innocent IV deaf to anything Frederick more honest than Innocent. but extirpation of the whole viper's brood. Personally Frederick and Innocent were not ill matched as combatants. As regards diplomatic morality, if these two terms can be coupled, it was diamond cut diamond. But circumstances made Frederick the more scrupulous, the more honest of the pair ; he wanted peace as badly as his Prussian namesake in the thick of the Seven Years' War. But all the same, what the Empire stood for was force and militarism ; its watchwords at best were order, ancient rights, Roman Law, But the Papacy still stood for the higher ideals ; absolutism. The watchwords of the Church were a higher kind of order, duties above rights, voluntary submission to God's law. What it professed to stand for was the higher side of life ; its message to be that of the Prince of Peace, its weapons solely spiritual. The victory over the Empire fell to the Papacy because the Papacy not merely represented the temporal policy of a succession of astute Italian nobles, but also still had its great spiritual function and represented the whole Church.

Both Empire and Papacy embodied a true unity among the nations of Christendom, but the latter was unity in a deeper sense, and for this reason the Papacy won and deserved to win. Of the two men Frederick had almost the whole right on his side in the immediate circumstances of the struggle, but when we have admitted Innocent's immediate aim to be a pernicious illusion, and his means to be both irreligious and immoral, we must yet recognize that behind him were ranged greater religious and moral forces than the Empire could muster. He won by the past of the Papacy, but at the cost of its future.

I have said that the Empire might have lasted several generations more. A fair trial would then have been given to the most interesting experiment that history contains of a government unique among governments between the fall of Rome and the seventeenth century, being highly centralized and rigorous as to justice and good order, and at the same time economically prosperous and tolerant to other religions. For such was the government which Frederick himself planned out and began for the two Sicilies in 1235. Again, we cannot but regret that the union of European states, however incomplete, was shattered by

yet, but for Innocent IV, the Empire might have lasted awhile, combining order and toleration,

and con- external causes before its time. For this potent
tinuing
the union conception, the unity of Christendom, was still
of Chris- capable of producing vast effects ; so tenacious
tendom.
of life was it that not even with the fall of the
Hohenstaufen could the Empire die, though it
was a shorn and parcelled Empire that lived on
under Hapsburgs, Luxemburgs, and Wittelsbachs.
Thirdly, we must allow that it was a beautiful
and ennobling vision which the mediaeval mind
imagined when it dreamed of the Caesar and the
Apostle seated side by side, the two great powers
working in harmony to carry out God's will upon
earth.

If it was but a vision it was one of those which
come through the ivory gate to elevate and to
purify an age, and to give it the inspiration which
can only come from an inward ideal.

LECTURE VI

THE POLICY OF INNOCENT IV IN SICILY AND IN GERMANY. HIS CHARACTER AND ULTIMATE INFLUENCE

CONRAD'S will had two startling clauses.[1] It committed his infant son Conradin ' to the hands of the Church '. It committed the regency of Sicily to the Marquis Berthold, the chief man among the German officials and captains now in south Italy. Each of these bequests, and especially the latter, practically made the Pope supreme arbiter of the situation. Thoroughly grasping this fact, he saw that his strength was to sit still. He had just concluded the unfortunate arrangement with Henry III, or rather he had empowered his envoy Albert to conclude it.[2] The resources of his diplomacy were quite equal to cashiering this arrangement, but all in good time, there was no need for indecorous haste. It would be almost August before he could hear exactly how the business stood. But his mind had at once reverted to his darling plan, the complete incorporation of Sicily with the Papal states. He received Berthold's embassy graciously in mid-July, but ' told them flatly he meant to have possession of the kingdom,

(marginal note: Papal position in May 1254.*)*

(marginal note: Innocent resumes his plan for Sicily.*)*

---

[1] B. F. W., *Regesta Imperii*, 4632, 4632ᵃ.
[2] Mon. Germ., *Epist. Pontif.* iii. 409.

and be lord of it, promising for Conradin when
he should come of age that he should have grace
done him as regarded his rights, if any, in the
kingdom '.[1] After fourteen days' negotiations the
treaty was suddenly broken off. The envoys
' walked fraudulently and had not the fear of God
before their eyes ', is the version of the faithful
Nicholas. But when this biographer breaks into
abuse of the other side, it always means that his
own case presents something awkward to cover up.
The fact is that by August, Innocent had heard
two pieces of news. One was that his envoy had
withheld the final ratification of the agreement
with Henry III. ' The king ' (he says) ' impor-
tuned me in season and out of season. But I saw
his helplessness. I knew the aid must come soon
to be of any use at all. So I refused to redraft
the agreement, and left matters where they were.' [2]
This does not quite concur with the view Henry
took, for it is clear that he regarded the matter
as practically settled, and himself as free to confer
Sicilian estates at least on paper.[3] But this constituted a most convenient situation, that Henry
should feel himself bound while the Papacy should
feel itself legally unfettered.

Rising in
Sicily,
its mean-
ing.
     The other gratifying news was the information
of the rising tide of feeling in Sicily against Berthold
and his Germans. There was something of national

---

[1] Jamsilla, 507 E ; also B. F. W. 4643ᵉ.
[2] *Epist. Pontif.* iii. 411.   [3] Rymer, i. 308, 310.

feeling in it, for the rule of the Rogers and
Frederick II had developed an unmistakable consciousness of unity among all the varied elements
of the two Sicilies. But there were other motives
in it too ; there was jealousy of the powerful
native bureaucracy against German arrogance and
greed, there was a revival of the ineradicable
traditions of autonomy on the part of the cities,
there was a recrudescence of the unconquerable
feudal instincts of the nobles. And behind all
this, inspiring, urging, controlling them, must have
been the powerful, ubiquitous, silent working of
the Church. The Pope had sent out no Legate ;
he had issued no manifesto ; but he had moved
down to Anagni to be within reach, to quote his
own words, and he knew that the Sicilian kingdom
which was written on his own heart was also an
object of ardent hope to all true sons of the Church.[1]
His plan was identical with that conceived by
Innocent III on the death of Henry VI ; Sicily
for the Sicilians, under Church governorship. It
was not an appeal to nationalism in the full modern
sense, for German troops fought under the Papal
banner as well as against it ; and to the men of
the south, officials from Rome would be almost as
distasteful as from across the Alps. But the movement was at any rate one of surprising vehemence
and unanimity. Innocent threw into it all the
tireless energy, all the boundless resourcefulness,

[1] His own words in *Epist. Pontif.* iii. 277.

F f

which had marked the Council of Lyons and
the year after Frederick's death.   The record of
this his last half-year is almost monopolized by
Sicilian documents.   All foreign holders of Sicilian
fiefs were to get investiture from the Holy See
by September 8, or suffer forfeiture.[1]   A host was
collected by preaching a Crusade in Italy, and was
put under the command of his nephew Cardinal
William Fieschi, as Legate, with the old soldier
Albert Fieschi at his right hand.   The fullest
powers, both temporal and ecclesiastical, were
conferred on the Legate, with a formula never
used on any other occasion by Innocent, ' all the
powers we should have ourselves if we were present
on the spot in person.' [2]   He was even to mark
the new Papal rule by issuing from the mint
a new coinage.   But before this host could gather,
already by mid-August the national revolt was so
universal that in the face of it Berthold resigned.

Submis-
sion of
Manfred.

Manfred, who had probably commended himself to
Papal favour when he was a member of Berthold's
embassy, was at first made regent for Conradin,
but was then induced to submit to Rome, Conradin's rights being guaranteed, and Manfred
himself appointed vicar from Faro to the Bay
of Amalfi[3] with a munificent salary of 800 gold
ounces and the fief of Taranto, and the others as
in Frederick's will.   When Innocent crossed the
Garigliano frontier to take possession of the

[1] *Epist. Pontif.* iii. 283.   [2] Ibid. 285.   [3] Ibid. 287, 289.

kingdom that he had won at last, he was met by
Manfred, who respectfully held the bridle for him.
It was natural that he should assume that he
could dispose at his will of this young man who
had been so submissive to him, so submissive to
Berthold and to Conrad, just as he had disposed
of Edmund of England, and as he had relegated
Conradin's claims to a convenient futurity. But
he made one fatal error, and that the most fatal
of all ; the selfsame error which was fatal to the
genius of a Julius Caesar and a Napoleon. He
despised those whom he had trampled on. The Inno-
contemptuous way in which, to reward partisans, mistake
estates were granted away which had just about Manfred.
been guaranteed to him, must have opened to
Manfred's eyes the gulf on the edge of which he
was standing, and must have warned him that
he too would be flung aside as soon as he had
served a purpose. It was only ten days later[1]
that Manfred found an armed ambush laid for him
by a personal enemy who was high in Papal favour.
In the scuffle that ensued the man was slain, and
the Pope at once declared Calabria forfeit. Nothing
was left for Manfred but to raise the standard of
revolt. Pliable and confiding as he had been when
the weapons were those of diplomacy, now that it
came to action and the field of warfare he proved
himself a true son of the great Emperor. He threw
himself on the loyalty of the Saracen troops[2] at

[1] 18 October, *Regesta,* 4644[f].   [2] *Regesta,* 4644[q].

Manfred Luceria. They rallied enthusiastically round the
escapes. prince who spoke their tongue, they swept aside
their own treacherous commandant and handed
over to Manfred the Imperial treasure. This was
on November 2. Innocent's feverish activity
during the next month is the concentration of
every energy, every resource, by one who sees all
his work falling into ruins about him, but who
means if he cannot win, at least to fight to the
end. For though the bishops and the cities
remained faithful to a rule which promised them
independence, yet the barons and mass of the
people had no liking for the idea of a priest-king,
and they flocked to Manfred's banner,[1] even those
who had cried for Papal intervention against the
Inno- Germans before. Amid such a crisis the Pope's
cent's unflinching tenacity of purpose has something
des-
perate which, had the cause been a better one, we might
energy. call sublime. To retain the cities, he renewed the
assurance that they should never be under any
but direct Papal rule.[2] Yet in the same breath
he renewed the negotiation with Henry III [3] as
if nothing had interrupted it, for English gold and
English credit were the only source from which
he could feed the army in Apulia now under the
Cross Keys. That the pledges to the cities and
the pledge to young Edmund of England were

---

[1] M. Paris, v. 460.

[2] *Epist. Pontif.* iii. 354, Nos. 394, 396, 411.

[3] Rymer, i. 312.

diametrically contradictory troubled him not at
all. With him, diplomacy had always been the
art of untying the knots itself had tied, and he
had always had two alternative means to his end.
So shrewd a judge of men must have appreciated
that Henry was not the king to carry out an
enterprise from which Charles of Anjou had shrunk.
But even the shrewdness of Innocent IV fell into
the usual Italian estimate of English wealth as
a reservoir at once accessible and inexhaustible,
and the usual Italian contempt for English gulli-
bility. He was right in thinking it would be easy
when the time should come for it to throw aside
Henry as a squeezed orange, but wrong in thinking
that the squeezing could yield an unlimited amount.
But probably he trusted that the time of need
would be over soon, that he would ride out this
storm as he had so many before. He still held
the larger half of the kingdom and the larger
army. Thus the news that came to him, ill and Man-
overwrought as he had long been, was a fatal fred's victory.
shock.[1] Manfred had won a great victory at
Foggia on December 2. The army of the Keys,
the 'Crusaders' led by the Pope's own nephew,
had broken up in panic and cowardly surrender.
It had melted into the rabble of which it had been
compounded. The 'Sultan of Nocera' was absolute master of the Church's kingdom.

For ten years all Innocent's plans had centred

[1] M. Paris, v. 471.

on one subject. They had been carried out with
a forethought that resembled divination, with
unexampled tactical skill, and with a resolution
that amounted to heroism. He had lavished on
this object the utmost resources of the Church,
illimitable as they might seem to be ; he had
sacrificed to it her spiritual character and her hold
on the future ; he had sacrificed his own conscience and reputation. It was, he avowed, the
thing nearest to his heart. Now, when at last
after innumerable disappointments he stretched
forth his hands confidently to grasp it, it slipped
from him like something in a dream. For the
fourth time in seven years the cup was dashed
aside as he raised it to his lips. He had meant
his pontificate to be the fulfilment and the fruition
of two of the chief ideas of his great namesake
and predecessor. The two boldest conceptions of
Innocent III, the conception of a territorial Papal
state, and the conception of a union of temporal
and spiritual dominion in one hand, were to have
been combined together and realized on a large
scale by Innocent IV. It was a glittering prospect
that had again and again during the last sixty
years opened out before the statesmen of the
Lateran ; or rather an *ignis fatuus* which had
lured them aside from their true work, and from
the vast sphere of beneficent influence awaiting
them ; a temptation characteristic of the Middle
Ages in that it offered to the Roman Church all

the kingdoms of the earth and the glory of them, but at the price of her own soul.

Such a sudden irremediable collapse, such a humiliation inflicted by a youth he had despised, and due to the folly of the one nephew of his own whom he had entrusted with high powers, might well break the heart even of Sinibald Fieschi. Like the battle in which Greek freedom fell, it must have killed with report. The news could not have come to him before December 5, and on December 7 he was dead.[1]

With his dying breath he adjured the cardinals The Pa- to continue the war. Alexander IV had been kept pacy con- in the background by his self-willed predecessor, tinues and the policy thus bequeathed was alien both to policy, his ideals, which were more spiritual, and to his temperament, which was more indolent. But he could not shake off the burden. The shade of Innocent seemed still to hang over the Papacy, as it plunged ever deeper into conflict with the Sicilian king, and ever deeper into humiliation, till at last it was only saved, as he had been, by the friendly intervention of death. Had not Manfred and Conradin successively fallen on the battle-fields of Benevento and Tagliacozzo, nothing could have rescued the Papacy from a Sicilian yoke. Even so it only escaped by substituting the yoke and so of a French cadet line ; and the golden prize, the falls cap- incorporation of the two Sicilies with the Papal France.

[1] Nicolas de Curbio, c. 43.

States, was further off than ever. Incidentally the
Angevin connexion led within a generation to what
has been well called the Seventy Years' Captivity
at Avignon. The Papacy had rooted out the
greatest dynasty in history, only to find itself
bound to the chariot wheels of France. Was this
a result for which it was worth while to have
dragged in the mire the Church of Anselm, Bernard,
and Francis ; to have ruined the loftiest ideal ever
essayed by man, the kingdom of God upon earth ?

Where we endeavour to draw out a sequence of
scientific causation, a far-reaching chain of logical
results, the mediaeval historians threw their
thoughts into a dramatic form, a vision of judgement. The literary and artistic form perhaps
contains as much essential truth as the modern
attempt to be scientific and philosophical.

This is the form in which the verdict of England
is presented by Matthew Paris.[1]

' In the week that Innocent IV died, one of the cardinals
had a vision by night. He seemed to be in heaven before
the tribunal of the Lord, on Whose right hand stood the
Virgin Mother, on His left, a matron of noble form and
rich attire, who bore in one hand a model which was
inscribed in letters of gold, " The Church." When Innocent knelt before the throne and with clasped hands
prayed for pardon, not judgement, that noble lady spoke
against him: "Oh, just Judge, give judgement righteously.
I accuse that man for three things. First, that whereas
thou didst found the Church and endow it with liberties,

[1] M. Paris, v. 471–2.

he has made her a wretched handmaid. Second, that whereas the Church was founded as the salvation of sinners, that it might win the souls of the wretched, he has made her a table of money-changers. Third, that whereas the Church was founded in faith, justice, and truth, he has made faith and morals waver, he has subverted justice, he has put out the light of truth. Therefore I say, render me just judgement." Then saith the Lord to him, " Go and receive reward according to thy deserts." And therewith he was taken forth.'

In the Classical Age and in the Age of the Renaissance men saw in catastrophes like these the work of Fortune, the capricious play of a mocking and even malicious power ; *voluit Fortuna iocari*. In the Middle Ages men saw in such catastrophes the manifest Hand of God ; *iudicia Dei abyssus*. History in our days feels no temptation to explain the world as the sport of chance, but she has also become chary of drawing moral lessons from every fall of a tower of Siloam. If one must try to express in a phrase the abiding impression left by a study of Papal activity during the period which opens with the accession of Innocent III, and closes with the death of Innocent IV, one might find it in the words with which that greatest of all Popes himself gave judgement on this territorial policy, ' Whoso touches pitch is defiled thereby.' [1] Might we not even think upon that great text, ' My kingdom is not of this world ' ?

We have seen the effect of Innocent's policy in

[1] *Gesta Inn.*, c. 18, in Muratori, *Ss.* iii. 489.

France and in England.　It is well to take a view
of its working in Germany.

Inno-
cent's
dealings
with the
German
Church;

'The stars shall fall from heaven, the rivers
turn to blood, sooner than the Pope abandon his
purpose.'　This was the word that went forth from
Lyons.　The purpose was war to the death in
Germany.　Let us see what were the weapons.
The first was the German episcopate.　Under
Barbarossa they had been state officials.　Innocent III had transformed them into an independent
hierarchy.　Gregory IX tried intimidation, but

the
bishops;

Innocent IV appealed to mundane motives, local
associations, individual interests.　No Church
principle, no Church property was allowed to
stand in the way of securing one of these new
proselytes.[1]　He had only to ask and have.　The
Bishop of Liege was allowed for twenty-seven
years to go on without taking orders at all, though
he was bound by oath to his chapter to do so.　We
ask why was this allowed?　He was brother of
the Count of Geldern, an important recruit.　All

'irregu-
larities',

manner of 'irregularities', that is, slaughterings,
plunderings, and burnings, were pardoned in
Papalist clerics.　For them, the rule against 'priests'
brats' in orders had no terrors.　Any one who
would serve against Conrad, who was befriended
by some leading Papalist, who was powerful enough
to be worth winning over, found no prohibited
degrees to any marriage, no cause or impediment

[1] Papal Registers, *passim.*

to any match. If the keeping of an oath 'would
redound to the disadvantage of the cause of the
Church', absolution was openly given on this
ground, or to reward an adherent or retain a
waverer. Other supporters were secured by the
simplest of all considerations, cash down ; one-
fifth of all Church revenues for a year, or all
vacancies for five years, or moneys levied for
Crusade. Churches were saddled with soldiers'
pay, with Papalist leaders' expenses, with com-
pensation of damage done by the Imperialists. The
whole German Church in ways almost countless
was made into a vast war-treasury. No see or
abbey was so influential, no parish priest so poor
as to escape. At every Church ceremony the
anathema by bell and candle was preached against
'Frederick, late Emperor'. Every fortnight the Crusade
Crusade was preached against him, to the furthest vows,
mission stations of the Baltic. Crusaders for the
Holy Land were to be turned back for this holier
war at home, four weeks' service in which earned
as much indulgence as a Crusade to Jerusalem.
Every place that failed to join in this was put
under Interdict. By Christmas 1245 the last
priest ceased officiating in Worms. Six months
later at least eighteen bishops and abbots were
under excommunication, and others deposed.
There was a great 'purging', too, of the chapters. purging
Clergy were deprived because their relatives, or the chapters,
the patrons of the livings, were Imperialists. In

November 1247 by one fell sweep *all* prelates who
provisions, had not yielded were summoned to Lyons. By
one stroke (September 1246) the Pope reserved to
himself all episcopal elections, and in 1249 all
abbeys. In 1248 in the one chapter of Constance
eighteen prebends were granted to Papal provisors.
pluralities, The dispensations to hold pluralities are counted
by hundreds. Between 1245 and 1250 twenty-
nine out of the fifty-four German sees were filled
' the by Papal nominees. Now we see what Innocent IV
spiritual sword,' had meant when he told the Cistercians he meant
to fight Frederick with ' the spiritual sword '.
There was indeed a hideous sincerity in his boast.
Everything spiritual, everything religious, became
a means to one political end. The revenues and
offices of the Church, its disciplinary and penitential system, its highest ideal of the Cross, its
lowest pecuniary motives, its very sacraments, were
forged into weapons. From this prostitution Papal
policy was never hereafter to shake itself free.

This degradation of the German Church, its
ruthless conversion into an agency of temporal
warfare, produced a deep resentment not only
among German laity, but among the finer minds
resent- of the clergy. The lay feeling had already expressed
ment of laity itself in the interesting poem of the minnesinger
Freidank, ' The two swords go not into one sheath.'
and the The clerical feeling comes out in four documents ;
clergy. first, in the Peacock, a bitter satirical poem on the
Council of Lyons ; second, in a strange mystical

appeal from a Dominican friar, one Arnold, to the
laity and the secular powers against the hierarchy
and that perverter of the Church and the Gospel,
Innocent IV ; third, in a call to all princes to
reform the Church and recover the temporal sword;
fourth, in an academic demonstration in complete
syllogistic form, that Innocenscius Papa adds up
to 666, the number of the Beast, and he is therefore
the Antichrist. These four survivals of what was
doubtless a copious literature show the revolt not
merely among the upper clergy and the universities
and the advanced mystical party, but even among
the friars themselves, the standing army of the
Papacy. And there is evidence of the same feeling
in the Cistercian order.

This is what Innocent IV did for the German
Church. Is this a victory ?

The reputation for cunning and tenacity which Personal
the ancient writers ascribed to the Piedmontese [1] charac-
has never ceased to be applicable to them. In Inno-
the Middle Ages the Genoese in particular were cent IV.
reckoned to be hard men of business even in
comparison with the traders of Venice, Pisa, or
Marseilles. Sinibald Fieschi was a typical Genoese,
and was regarded as such by his compatriots. At
the same time he had the qualities of that Piedmontese nobility, to which his family, the Counts
of Lavagna, belonged ; intense family pride, cold
unwavering materialism ; a vengefulness that,

[1] ' Haud Ligurum extremus dum fallere fata sinebant.'

once aroused, never slumbered, never forgot, but pursued beyond the grave. His high birth gave him a just self-confidence and a social tact that had early marked him out for diplomatic missions ; these, in turn, gave him knowledge of the world and a wide knowledge of human character, at least upon the seamy sides. He had the Italian courtesy and grace of manners, the Italian show of spontaneity and even gaiety that have so often captivated and befooled the 'barbarians'. He had all the Italian respect for decorum, ceremony, the externals of life. No one ever saw him dress or behave or speak in any way obviously unbecoming to his order or his high office. No one could pour scorn on him, as they had on his predecessors, for bursts of passion or for extravagances uttered *His rela-* in convivial intercourse. Nor did he make *tion to* Gregory IX's or Innocent III's mistake of being *the car-* *dinals.* domineering with the cardinals. Not that he was free, any more than they had been, from critics and opponents within the College. But he listened to all, he let them try their own way. He abstained even from predicting their failure, though he was quite ready to ensure it if things turned out unexpectedly feasible for them, as when he threw over his own legates and fled from Sutri in 1244 to escape from an imminent treaty. By this apparent open-mindedness, he avoided the scandal of scenes between the Holy Father and his brethren such as had shocked the faithful and offered a leverage to the enemy, even under Innocent III. Innocent IV's cardinals were two-thirds of them his own creations, without ever being allowed to rise to a position of favouritism ; but he let them share freely in the wealth that flowed into the Curia, and he rewarded good service bountifully, nor ever wantonly rebuked or revoked or discredited his legates : hence no Pope was better served, or more the master in his own house. It was he who instituted for the cardinals their red hats, to be an outward sign and reminder that they were to be ready to shed their blood for the Church.

Yet it is doubtful if any one felt affection for him, or he for any one. His munificence was calculation rather than generosity ; it was not from the heart but from the head, the broad view of the merchant prince who knows that it pays to pay well. Even his nepotism was not from the His nepotism. ordinary motives any more than it was confined within the ordinary limits. He gave on a lavish scale to his relatives, partly that they might be the better equipped for his service ; partly because he preferred men on whom he could depend as being nobodies without him ; partly perhaps from the strong Italian sense of the ' casa ', the group of expectant kinsmen. He found good places for a brother and for eight nephews to whom he was now the universal provider. But he was far above the vulgar weakness of pushing them into functions to which they were not equal. His relatives had no influence upon his policy; they were his instruments, never his inspirers or his guides. His legates, except in the one case of William Fieschi, 1254, were selected by fitness, not by family interest, and were expected to be successful.

Comparison with his three predecessors.
His three predecessors in the Papacy were, each in his own way, far superior to him; Innocent III in greatness of soul, Honorius III in moral goodness, Gregory IX in fiery vehemence. But all three had failed to achieve the goal of supremacy for the spiritual over the secular power. This achievement was reserved for him who had none of this greatness of soul, none of this moral goodness, and who above all eschewed fire and vehemence, and was simply practical. He seemed to have laid to heart a lesson from each of the three. The Pope who was to win must not aim too high, but must confine himself to what was within his grasp; he must realize that not goodness but self-interest dominates in mundane things; he must never be in a hurry nor make an enemy unnecessarily. Thus, firstly, he moves to the goal

His foresight.
step by step, making good each foot of ground before proceeding to the next; his measures working out in an orderly sequence as of a great plan of campaign which unfolds itself with logical fatality, because each move in it has been thought out long beforehand. Secondly, he relies not on

His worldly wisdom.
any great religious idea, not on traditional ecclesi-

astical tactics, but on common motives of the world, the desire of office, land, money ; he turns everything to its material use ; whatever is expedient, is lawful ; oaths and vows, indulgences and absolutions and dispensations, benefices and tithes, Heaven itself and Hell, are all converted into the sinews of war. The cause sanctifies all that is done for it. Canonical rules, moral principles, legal sanctions, all go by the board and are cut adrift when ' St. Peter's bark is tossing in the storm '. Thirdly, he is never out of heart or out of temper ; he never gives needless offence, or forgets that he who is to-day an adversary may to-morrow be an ally. He knows that he must take men as he finds them, and that violent language only weakens a case, and that violent measures are apt to stiffen neutrals into declared foes. It is this marvellous patience that gives him the courage to open a campaign with such slender resources as he seemed to muster in the autumn of 1244, and to maintain it with such composure in a crisis as in the spring of 1247 ; to postpone an advance till the time is ripe, as it was for the move on Sicily in May 1254 ; to endure with perfect equanimity such persistent recalcitrancy as that of the German lay princes up to 1251 ; to reject ostensibly no mediation however futile he meant to make it, as he did with the Count of Toulouse, the two Patriarchs, the King of France. Then when his hour at last came, this calm inflexible nature assumes a terrible

His self-control.

aspect, and has something about it of more or less than human. The sentence on the Staufen in 1248, when at last all reserve can be thrown off, is absolute, final, irrevocable ; neither Frederick nor son or descendant of his is to rule as Emperor or King on any terms ; the brood of vipers is to be exterminated. ' The stars might fall from heaven and the rivers turn to blood,' he said, ' but this word should not be taken back.' [1]

A man of business. The greatest power on earth was at last in the hands of a consummate man of business—that is, one who combined perfect clearness of plans and boldness in setting them going, with the keenest practical sense of the means required ; and an unconquerable tenacity in the execution of them by those means. The very day of his election he struck the key-note of his pontificate ; he called together his brethren the cardinals to discuss the measures needed to secure the peace of the Church and to deal with the Emperor. These were the expressions ever on his lips. He would show that his one object was a lasting peace for the Church ; his one principle to act through and with the cardinals ; his one preoccupation the Emperor.

Evidence of the Registers. He set to work with a tireless diligence that makes his registers an overwhelming monument. Nothing escapes him, from Iceland to Tunis, from the pillars of Hercules to the land of the Tartars. Nothing is too little ; nothing is beneath his

[1] *Epist. Pontif.* iii. 406.

attention ; every one is worth cultivating ; everything will come in useful some day. He is full of
enterprise and not afraid to throw himself into
a new set of circumstances. No conjuncture finds His
him unprepared. The most diverse forces and power of adapta-
impulses of that motley time are all welcome to tion.
him, because he knows how to avail himself of
each. He is as much at home in a summer's
retreat among the pious friars of Assisi as in a six
years' residence in the armed camp of Lyons ; in
a Cistercian chapter at Cluny as in the tumultuous
civic receptions at Genoa, Milan, and Bologna ;
in secret conclave with St. Louis or in stormy
interviews with Brancaleone and the republicans
of Rome. From each he can extract the one
quality they have in common for his purpose, the
concentration and focusing of all elements of
opposition to the Empire.

Business methods applied to politics are what is His
euphemistically called diplomacy; and Innocent IV diplo- macy.
had full command of the arts of the diploma-
tist. No one knew better how to deceive without
lying ; though from this latter, too, he did not
shrink on occasion, as in the peace negotiations of
1244, or when he assured Azzo of Este that there
had been no peace negotiations in 1247. But it
often sufficed to let a false impression go uncon-
tradicted, such as the impression that his flight
from Genoa was to escape not from his own
promises and his own plenipotentiaries, but from

threatened personal violence ; or the impression
that Frederick was not sincere about peace in
1245. He knew also how to keep the benefits of
an act which he had reprobated, as in the surrender
at Viterbo ; and how to let others do the dirty
work, as in the murder plot of 1246–7, or in the
scurrilous pamphlets which circulated freely among
the assembled fathers at Lyons. The biography
gives a very unpleasing reflection of the sort of
statements that were put about in the confidential
circle nearest to the Pope ; such as that Frederick
sent Christian virgins as presents to the Sultan,
that he lived and consorted wholly with Saracens,
that he pulled down a church to build privies on
the site of the high altar, that he poisoned Louis of
Thuringia and sent the assassin who slew Louis
of Bavaria, that he not only committed but openly
advocated unnatural sins, that his death-bed was
a scene of frenzied torments and blaspheming
despair, and so on through a long list of statements
of equal value with these. Unfortunately for the
biographer he could not be aware that documents
were extant and would be preserved which absolutely disprove some of the charges where he
rashly committed himself to definiteness, as when
he says that the Emperor denied supplies and the
use of his ports to the French king while on
Crusade, whereas five official orders from Frederick
and several letters of thanks from Louis prove the
exact contrary.

Innocent had too good a command of the science of the game to allow himself often to be forced into that last resource of diplomacy, a revoke. But even a repudiation of engagements he was prepared to commit if necessary. Thus he threw over the assurances given as to recalling Geoffrey of Montelongo in 1243, and the promises made by his legate to Jesi in 1248. At the other end of the diplomatic scale is the maxim, not to show one's hand prematurely. His biographer notices how ' benignly ' the Pope received advances even from Conrad, from Manfred, from the rebellious Romans. He felt so sure of himself and of his own strength.

One of the greatest difficulties in the way of powerful rulers has always been the selecting and the controlling of their instruments. But Innocent IV had a keen eye for character. He discerned exactly which men to employ for which work, and could find how to get the best out of a passionate partisan like Rainer of Viterbo, an honourable and well-meaning respectability like Cardinal Otto, a ' son of Belial ' like Philip of Ferrara. In each case he did justice to their qualifications, but recognized their limitations. Hence no success made him exaggerate what an agent could do, or tempted him to confer more powers than he had at first designed, or led him into dangerous impulses of gratitude. No subordinate could force his hand or dazzle his judgement. Cardinal Rinaldo of Ostia, though of high birth and much influence, was fat .

His choice of agents.

and lazy, so he left him behind in 1244. Geoffrey of Montelongo was a scandalous ruffian, but a first-class fighting man and a power among his Lombard compatriots ; so to the wars in Lombardy he was kept despite his petitions for release. Albert Behaim was as hot of tongue and hot of head as he was greedy, but his zeal and his Bavarian connexions were useful, so he was removed from Germany and kept at Lyons as an underling and a go-between. The Pope's own chaplain and confessor was only rewarded with a bishopric at Assisi, and that after many years' devotion. Rainer, who did such yeoman service in the Papal State, was never raised above the cardinal diaconate he held before. The legates in Germany were none of them entrusted with a long term of office ; the frequent changes enabled the Pope to keep the strings well in his own hand. He had no more hesitation in shifting and superseding them than a commander-in-chief would have in elevating a younger and more capable general over the heads of others. Thus when in August 1248 he saw the hour had struck for the long-cherished move upon Sicily, he would not commit so great an enterprise to any of the ' old gang ' who had borne the burden and heat of affairs in mid-Italy for five years past. With suave apologies to Cardinal Rinaldo of Ostia, on whom he could not think of laying so grievous a load, to Cardinals Stephen and Richard, and with no apology at all to Cardinal Rainer of Viterbo, he

passed them all over for the newer man, the son
of a Roman citizen, Peter Capocci, cardinal of
St. George, who had just been so wonderfully
successful in Germany. Him he summoned in
haste, November 1248, and conferred on him
unprecedented powers. He was not afraid to
back his own estimate of a man, and he was
rarely deceived in it.

It was quite in keeping with Innocent's self-
contained and self-sufficing nature that he fully
understood the weaknesses of men and made these
too subserve his purposes. He could be a courtly
and splendid host. His great entertainments at
Lyons are often recounted admiringly. He entered
readily into all the pomp and show that made his
return from Lyons one long triumphal progress.
At his departure from Lyons the crowd was too
vast for any one building, so he held a grand
ceremonial of farewell, and gave them his benediction in the fields outside. He allowed himself to
be escorted into the cities under a baldacchino
supported by the nobles. At Milan he passed
through jubilant multitudes for ten miles, and
never all the way failed in condescension. Milan
might well rejoice, as the onlooker says,[1] with
a joy indescribable, for after twenty-four years of
stubborn struggle, and many a day of darkness
and despair, she had won her heart's longing, and
was free to plunge into that desirable saturnalia

His use
of men's
weak-
nesses.

---

[1] Nic. de Curbio, c. 30, in Murat. *Ss.* iii. 592.

of anarchy which was to end in two centuries of stifling despotism followed by three and a half of degrading foreign thraldoms.

His use of the Friars.

Again, he fully grasped the importance of the new mendicant Orders. He had friars about him in his household. He made them the almoners of the systematic largesse by which he won over the turbulent population of Lyons during his seven years' stay. He was particularly cordial to Salimbene in 1247,[1] and to John of Parma, General of the Franciscans. He lived with them for months at Assisi ' like a brother among brethren '. He canonized one of them who had been murdered by the heretics in Lombardy. Very fittingly friars of both Orders watched his coffin after his death, as they had worked fanatically for him during his life.

He was well aware of the enthusiastic side of the religion of his day, though assuredly far enough from a sympathetic sharing in it. Accordingly he made much show of negotiations with the Emperor Vatatzes in 1254, as an ostensible step to securing the reconciliation of the Greek Church. He sent out two friars with full ecclesiastical equipment to complete the conversion of the Tartars, who were rumoured to be inclining towards Christianity. But these were official duties.

He put the Pa- pacy on

Innocent IV, the first Pope who was a con- summate man of business, was the first Pope to

---

[1] Salimbene, f. 284 ᶜ, &c.

admit without disguise that the Papacy must have a finan-
cial
basis. an adequate financial basis, and to perceive the vast potentialities of taxability in Christendom. A world-state as he conceived it could not be made a reality, could not be administered without laying the world under contribution. In this he displays his strong common sense. All his contemporaries realized that with him began a new era in the fiscal system of the Roman See. No doubt he knew well enough what bitter things about ' Romish avarice ' and the ' venality ' of the Curia would be said in many a monastery, and even lead to riots in many a land. But he knew too that taxation was always received with ignorant impatience, that hard words break no bones, and that monks and laymen must pay up in the end. His biographer computes that in the seven years' residence at Lyons, besides the ordinary expenses of the household, the court, the chancery, more than 200,000 marks (some three and a half million pounds in modern equivalent) were paid out for the struggle with the Empire.

' The richest of all the Popes since St. Peter,' ' The long delays and infinite cost of the Papal court,' these two notes sound over and over again in the chronicles. But they do not take into account the inevitableness of such a development. Quite apart from undertakings of a questionable character, the regular expenses of the Papacy could no longer be left dependent on casual offerings, semi-voluntary fees from suitors, and occasional levies of tithes, with territorial rents which were always in arrear. Innocent IV made all these sources of revenue fixed and regular, and added new sources. For instance, he empowered representatives present at his court to borrow large sums and pledge their abbeys at home as security. He backed up by spiritual sanctions the actions for the recovery of these loans. He entered into close relations with firms of bankers, Roman, Florentine, Siennese, and he had resident financial agents in the chief European capitals, merchants of our lord the Pope, as they called themselves. The Papacy had to be put on a business footing, like every other institution. No one was better fitted to accomplish such a task than this astute matter-of-fact Genoese. What revolted Christendom was that he brought the financial aspect into such repulsive prominence, that he drained the wells so dry, that he converted everything to such utterly secular objects.

Innocent was a canonist.
It is not easy for a man of affairs to be a man of general culture too. But there is one study at least of which he must feel the value, the study of law. Sinibald Fieschi was already famous for his knowledge of this subject, when he first attracted the notice of Honorius III in 1223, and made himself useful to the Legate Ugolino. As Pope he always had about him in his palace a school of theology and of canon law. Among canonist Popes

he ranks with Alexander III and Innocent III.[1]
Beyond this his intellectual interests did not go. His atti-
He does not seem to have touched at any point the tude to culture
literature or art of his age.   He spent no money and art
on fine buildings nor even on religious foundations.
He had the credit of starting at Lyons the rebuild-
ing of the Cathedral and the Rhone Bridge ; but
it was ages before either was completed, and his
share seems to have consisted chiefly in the offer
of indulgences to contributors.   His mind was
severely concentrated on his one absorbing object.
In this respect, as in so many others, he presents Com-
an utter contrast to Frederick II, that extraordi- pared with
narily varied and many-sided personality, which Frede-
reflected every aspect of his time and responded rick II.
to every impulse, which embodied every form of
culture, was full of the joy of life, of art, of
friendship, and which presents to us a nature that
if it sometimes repels, more often attracts, and is
always full of a strange fascination ; a nature so
powerful, rich, and manifold, that by contrast with
it the figure of the Pope is cold, narrow, unlovable,
even inhuman.   Yet at bottom they have qualities
in common.   In each there is the same swift clear
intelligence, the same power of dominating and
dwarfing those about them, the same matter-of-
fact appeal to men's interests, the same infinite
power of taking pains.   Both have boundless
patience, boundless confidence and resourcefulness.

[1] Schulte, *Gesch. d. canonischen Rechts*, ii. 91.

Each has one great purpose, and each is willing to advance towards it inch by inch, to sacrifice for it repose and health, and life itself. Frederick's belief in his destiny, in his imperial vocation to curb and rule Italy, is conspicuous.

His self-confidence. But Innocent had as strong a belief in the supremacy of the Holy See, and in its predestined triumph. 'The victory must needs come to the Church always.' This is what sustained him, so that hope radiated from him as from a pillar of fire when hope had gone out from all the rest. It was this that made him such that he never flagged, never forgot, never gave up. The stars in their courses fought for him. When Frederick was advancing to Lyons in 1247, the revolt of Parma came to save him. When Italy seemed lost in 1249, it was the capture of Enzio which changed the face of the sky. When, in 1250, his party in Germany was shattered, when his long-prepared attack on Sicily was a fiasco, when France herself had turned in wrath upon him, at each darkest hour of all the dawn appeared, as when the great Emperor himself had died a sudden death in 1250. 'Victory must needs come to the Church.' But

Was it a victory for the Church? had the Church really won? Was the victory of Innocent IV a victory for the Church? Was it even a victory for his own plans? He had taken the Church at her highest and best, in the climax of the thirteenth century, that glorious flowering-time of the Middle Ages, and in eleven years had destroyed half her power for good, and had launched her irretrievably upon a downward course. He had crushed the greatest ruling dynasty since the Caesars, and ruined the greatest attempt at government since the fall of Rome. In ruining the Empire, he had ruined also the future of the Papacy. Was this a victory ?

Dante puts in the black starless air of the outer circle of the Inferno the shade of him *che fece lo gran rifiuto*. Of all Dante's tremendous verdicts, none has such a bitter ring of scorn as this. It is generally interpreted of one individual Pope ; but it might well stand as judgement on the whole Papacy of the thirteenth century, when it bartered spiritual leadership for temporal rule, the legacy of St. Peter for the fatal dower of Constantine.

OXFORD: HORACE HART M.A.
PRINTER TO THE UNIVERSITY

DATE DUE